LIVING TRUST

HOW TO SET UP A LIVING TRUST, PROTECT YOUR ASSETS, BYPASS PROBATE, SAVE BIG ON TAXES, AND SECURE YOUR FAMILY'S FUTURE WITHOUT EXPENSIVE LAWYERS OR COMPLICATED PAPERWORK

LUCAS STERLING

TOP TIER PRESS

Published under the author brand **Lucas Sterling**

CONTENTS

INTRODUCTION

Imagine a moment, years from now, when your family gathers to reflect on the life you built and the legacy you leave behind. In that quiet room, emotions run high—because loss always brings pain—but there's something else: clarity, order, and peace of mind. There are no frantic searches for paperwork, no marathon meetings with lawyers, and no endless waiting for courts to decide what happens next. Instead, your wishes are honored swiftly and smoothly. Assets move seamlessly to loved ones. The home you worked hard for remains in the family. Children and grandchildren receive their inheritance without strife or expense. There's relief at a time when it matters most. This future isn't just possible—it's closer than you think. And it starts with a simple document: the living trust.

Maybe you've heard about living trusts before or skimmed articles online. Perhaps a friend mentioned them in passing, or a financial advisor dropped the term into conversation. But if you're like millions of Americans, the world of estate planning still feels confusing and intimidating. Legal terms blur together. Probate sounds mysterious—something that only happens to other people, until it doesn't. It's not surprising: for decades, estate planning has been shrouded in jargon and treated as a luxury reserved for the wealthy. As a result, many middle-class families, regular homeowners, and well-intentioned parents delay planning, uncertain about where to start or how much it will cost.

The truth is, most people misunderstand what a living trust actually is. Some think it's only for the rich or those with complex business empires. Some think it's like a will or that it means giving up control of assets early. These myths persist because professional advice too often comes wrapped in complexity—with expensive hourly fees and intimidating forms. Yet a living trust is not a privilege of the wealthy, nor is it an instrument that takes away your autonomy. In its essence, a living trust is a legal arrangement that allows you to transfer ownership of your property, investments, and other assets into a trust that you control while you're alive. You can change or revoke it at any time. When you pass away, the successor you named steps in and distributes your assets directly to the people you care about most—bypassing costly court proceedings and minimizing potential disputes.

Why does this matter so much? Because failing to plan means leaving your legacy in the hands of strangers—judges, lawyers, and government officials who don't know your family or your intentions. Without a living trust, your loved ones will likely face probate, an expensive, public, and time-consuming court process required to validate your will and oversee the distribution of your assets. Probate is a roadblock at a time of grief. It routinely takes six months to a year—or longer—before heirs gain access to property and funds. Meanwhile, legal fees and administrative expenses can eat up five percent or more of your estate. Even simple estates aren't immune. Homes may need to be sold under pressure. Bank accounts can be frozen. Family businesses risk disruption or dissolution. Sibling disputes and blended family complications sometimes escalate into lasting rifts. Every year, court costs and legal battles divert billions of dollars intended for families due to a lack of timely planning.

A living trust may be the single most important document you ever create if you own a home, have children or grandchildren, or want to spare your loved ones unnecessary hardship. Unlike a standard will—which guarantees probate—a living trust ensures your legacy is handled privately, efficiently, and in line with your exact wishes. You retain full control of your assets throughout your life, with the freedom to buy, sell, refinance, or make changes whenever you choose. When the unexpected happens, your instructions remain clear, avoiding confusion and chaos for those left behind. For parents and grandparents, this means protecting children's inheritances until they are mature enough to handle them responsibly. For business owners, it means providing for uninterrupted leadership and the smooth transition of key assets. For those caring for aging parents, it offers a way to provide ongoing support, even if mental capacity diminishes. In blended families, it delivers clarity, equity, and fairness that everyone understands.

So why do so few people take this vital step? Fear and uncertainty often dominate the answer. The idea of confronting our mortality is daunting. The prospect of wading through legal paperwork is overwhelming, especially when so much is at stake. Many people fear making mistakes or falling victim to unethical advisors. Worst of all, some delay estate planning entirely—hoping that "one day" will suffice. Yet every day, ordinary families pay the price for that hesitation.

The good news is that setting up a living trust is far simpler and more affordable than you might imagine. With the right roadmap, you don't need a law degree—or even a lawyer—to put one in place. This book was written for individuals and families just like you: adults navigating the responsibilities of homeownership, parenthood, caregiving, or entrepreneurship; people who want clarity without complexity; and do-it-yourselfers who value actionable guidance over legalese. Inside, you'll find step-by-step instructions tailored for real life, using plain language and practical tools. I'll walk you through every stage of the process, from deciding whether a living trust makes sense for your circumstances to drafting key documents, funding your trust, and ensuring your wishes hold up over time. You'll learn how to avoid common pitfalls, sidestep needless expenses, and secure peace of mind for yourself and those you love most.

There's no sugarcoating the significance of these decisions or the comfort that comes from knowing your affairs are in order. A living trust is more than a legal document: it's a powerful act of love and responsibility. By taking action now, you dramatically simplify the path for your family during their most vulnerable moments. You eliminate barriers, preserve hard-earned assets, and shield your loved ones from bureaucratic headaches and emotional strain. Most importantly, you ensure the legacy you built endures long after you're gone—not just in material wealth, but in the security, dignity, and stability you provide.

Throughout the pages ahead, I'll demystify every facet of living trusts and estate planning, revealing options that fit a wide spectrum of needs—from modest homes to growing small businesses, from young professionals starting out to retirees looking for lasting security. Whether you're preparing for your own later years or helping a parent, partner, or adult child, you'll find the confidence to act and the knowledge to get it done right.

Your journey to a stronger legacy begins here. Let's remove the uncertainty, reduce the burden, and make sure your final gift to your loved ones is a future free from needless obstacles. No lawyer required—just the willingness to start today.

UNLOCK YOUR ESTATE PLANNING & LIVING TRUST COMPANION WORKBOOK

Ready to turn your estate planning goals into clarity, confidence, and lasting peace of mind?

As a thank-you for reading this book, I've created a helpful companion resource: **The Estate Planning & Living Trust Companion Workbook.** This practical guide helps you organize documents, define your legacy, and create a trust that reflects your values. It's designed to take you from uncertainty to assurance in just a few thoughtful steps.

What's included in this resource:

- Clarify your estate planning goals
- Organize and record key information and assets
- Simplify trust creation and beneficiary planning
- Protect your loved ones and ensure your wishes are honored

👉 **Access Your Companion Workbook**
Visit: **https://content.toptierpress.com/simplify-planning-journey**

Or scan the QR code below to get instant access!

CHAPTER 1

LIVING TRUST BASICS—WHAT YOU NEED TO KNOW BEFORE YOU START

Years ago, when my parents first began sorting through their estate plans, the complexity and uncertainty felt overwhelming. Terms like "trustee," "probate," and "beneficiary" were tossed around with little explanation, leaving important decisions tangled in confusion and delay. Watching their experience unfold revealed how common misunderstandings about living trusts often stand between families and smooth transitions.

Understanding the basics of living trusts—their purpose, key terms, how they differ from wills, and the real benefits they provide—can simplify a process that many find intimidating. This chapter lays the foundation for making informed choices by breaking down what living trusts are, why they matter, and how they help protect both your assets and your family's future.

Understanding Living Trusts and Essential Terms

A living trust is a legal tool that helps people manage and pass on their property without court delays or public involvement. It allows someone to put their assets, like homes or accounts, into a trust while alive so that after death, these assets move directly to the people chosen as beneficiaries. In basic terms, a living trust works like a special container. Instead of owning assets in your own name, you hold them through the trust. You set the rules, pick who manages everything, and decide who gets what when you die or become unable to handle things on your own.

Understanding the differences between a living trust and a will helps make things clearer. Both transfer assets to loved ones, but they do it in different ways. A will only goes into effect after you die. The will must go to probate court, which is a public legal process where a judge makes sure your instructions are followed. This can take months, and anyone can look up your will in public records. A living trust, by contrast, takes effect as soon as you sign and fund it. If you are alive but can't handle your affairs—say, because you're sick or injured—the trust lets someone else step in automatically. After your death, there is no probate for assets in the trust. Family members do not have to wait for court approval, and the process stays private.

Think of two common family examples. Joe and Rita, homeowners with grown children, have a will that names the kids as heirs. When Joe passes, everything owned in his name hits probate, even the house. The children have to wait until the judge approves the will and transfers the home. Rosie, instead, uses a living trust and puts the house and bank accounts in it while alive. Her children do not need court help. The successor trustee handles the paperwork, and her kids get the house smoothly.

Breaking down key terms builds confidence in handling these choices. A trust is a legal agreement where you give someone responsibility to manage what you own for another person's benefit. The living trust is a trust you set up while you are alive—meaning not in your will and not after your death. Most living trusts are revocable trusts, which means you can change or cancel the trust any time while you are alive and mentally alert. If you buy a new home or change your mind about who gets what, you don't need to start over.

The person who creates the trust is the grantor. Other common terms for this role are "settlor" or "trustor"—all mean the same person, the one putting property into the trust. The grantor keeps control if they name themselves as the initial trustee, which is very common. The trustee is the individual or company responsible for handling the trust according to your written instructions. If you are able, you serve as a trustee for your living trust. If something happens to you, the person you choose as successor trustee takes over management. This person follows your instructions, pays bills, handles final debts, and then gives out assets as you planned. The beneficiary is the person or group who receives the property or money from the trust, such as a spouse, children, grandchildren, or charity.

Imagine Alice, who owns a house and savings account. She makes a living trust, names herself as trustee, and moves her home and accounts into the trust's name. She names her daughter as a successor trustee and both of her children as beneficiaries. If Alice becomes sick and can't manage bills, her daughter starts acting as trustee right away. After Alice's death, her daughter follows the instructions: pays leftover bills and then gives the house to the brother and sister.

Common property that goes into living trusts includes real estate—like homes or cottages—bank accounts, savings, investment accounts, stocks, bonds, and valuable personal possessions. Some items, such as retirement accounts or life insurance, already pass directly through named beneficiaries, so they are not usually moved into the trust. A will is still useful if you want to name a guardian for minor children, or to transfer items not placed into the trust, such as a car or family heirlooms you did not retitle.

Making these choices gives practical benefits beyond just passing property. Living trusts offer privacy for the family, since there are no public court records. They also mean that managing or distributing assets does not have to wait for the courts, saving time and stress. This stronger control and privacy helps families take care of loved ones more smoothly, even when life takes an unexpected turn or health changes quickly. Now that the basics are clear, it becomes possible to see why setting up a living trust may be worth considering and how these benefits can make a difference for real families.

Exploring the Key Benefits of Living Trusts

Families often discover the true difference between a **will** and a **living trust** during difficult times—not when these documents are first created. While a will serves a clear and essential purpose, it also requires involvement with the probate court system. A living trust helps bypass that process, allowing you to transfer property privately, efficiently, and with greater control. Understanding how each tool functions gives you a real advantage when deciding what's best for the people you love.

Privacy: Keeping Family Matters Out of the Public Eye

Wills must go through probate court, which is an open, public process. Anyone can check court records and learn what assets are in an estate, who gets them, and even see disputes between family members. With a living trust, the details remain private. The only people who need to know are your chosen trustees and beneficiaries.

Picture a mother named Linda, whose wish is to leave her home and savings to her children after she dies. If she leaves these assets in a will, they become part of a public record, easily searchable in probate filings. Friends, neighbors, and even scam artists could see exactly what Linda owned and who inherited it. With a living trust, Linda's personal information and family details do not leave the living room. Only those named in the trust know how the inheritance is divided. Many people worry that complete privacy sounds unrealistic, especially in the digital age. In reality, a properly set up living trust offers a solid layer of protection from prying eyes.

Probate Avoidance: Faster, Simpler, and Less Stressful

Probate is more than just a word lawyers throw around. It is the legal process where the court reviews a will, deals with debts, and approves the distribution of assets. This takes months or even longer, often a year or more. In the meantime, family members may not have access to funds needed to pay bills, handle repairs, or settle urgent financial needs. They may also be required to attend multiple court dates, and the court may hold up asset transfers for reasons outside their control.

When a property is owned by a living trust, the probate process is skipped entirely. The assets are distributed by the person you choose, called your trustee, according to the rules set up in the trust. If a homeowner named Samuel places his house in a living trust, his spouse or children can take care of paperwork and transfer the title within weeks—not months or years. This is a relief for many, since grieving families are already facing enough pressure. A frequent worry is whether the trust will actually do what it promises—that is, let people avoid probate delays. The reality is, assuming the trust is funded (the assets are formally transferred into it), there are no courts involved and no waiting for a judge's approval.

Typical Timeline: Probate vs. Living Trust

- **Probate with a Will:** 6–18 months (possible court fees, delays, and paperwork)
- **Living Trust Distribution:** Usually 1–4 weeks (direct by trustee, minimal court involvement)

Personal Control: Deciding How and When Assets Are Shared

Wills usually leave assets all at once, so an 18-year-old might suddenly inherit a large sum, ready or not. Living trusts let you set clear conditions and schedules. You can give a portion of money when a child turns 21, another at 25, or tie later gifts to finishing college.

Imagine a parent, Roberta, who wants to help her teenage children but also wants to prevent misuse or waste. In her living trust, she can state that her son receives money every year for living expenses, but larger amounts are only released when certain life goals are met. A blended family, say two remarried parents with kids from earlier marriages, may want to be sure both their biological and stepchildren receive what is fair. With a trust, you write these instructions in detail, preventing confusion or future disagreement. Some people fear that such rules become too rigid or get ignored. As long as you name a responsible trustee and update the trust if life changes, your plan will be honored and enforced in the way you intend.

Why These Benefits Matter

Privacy allows families to avoid unwanted attention, embarrassment, or outside interference. **Bypassing probate** saves months of time, legal fees, and emotional strain when loved ones are already coping with loss. **Control over details**ensures that children and dependents are cared for and protected according to your wishes—guidance that continues even after you're gone. Each of these advantages helps families safeguard what matters most—not only in terms of money, but in peace of mind. Together, they make a **living trust** a powerful tool for shaping your legacy on your own terms.

Despite these strengths, misunderstandings about living trusts are common. Some people assume they're complicated to create or useful only for the wealthy. In truth, with a little guidance and a clear grasp of the key benefits, most families can establish a trust that fits their needs and removes much of the confusion surrounding estate planning.

Addressing Common Misconceptions and Fears

The privacy, flexibility, and probate-skipping features of living trusts catch the attention of adults wanting to protect their assets or streamline matters for their families. But almost as soon as people hear about the upsides, a mix of caution and skepticism often sets in. The old saying "too good to be true" echoes in many minds, especially with something as serious as legal planning. Misconceptions and fears leave a real mark on decisions here, holding people back from making choices that could help them.

Living Trusts Are Only For The Wealthy

A top myth claims that living trusts are just for millionaires or people with sprawling portfolios. Many middle-income earners or homeowners hear that only the ultra-rich use trusts and assume it's not the right tool for them. The reality is that living trusts offer strong benefits to those who want privacy, want to avoid probate, and want to organize their affairs cleanly, no matter their overall wealth. For example, a married couple with a modest home worried their assets were too small for a trust. Their attorney demonstrated to them how costly probate proceedings could ensnare even a single-family home if left solely to a will. With a living trust, their property could pass privately and easily to their children, skipping court delays.

Anyone who owns property, has accounts with beneficiary designations, or wants to make things easier for their loved ones can use a living trust. It's not about net worth; it's about control and giving clear instructions that reduce headaches for families.

Living Trusts Are Complicated and Expensive

Complexity, or the fear of unintentionally making a mistake, halts many individuals. They picture piles of paperwork, high lawyer fees, and a process reserved for legal experts. Some estate planning advertisements even stoke this fear, making the trust process sound like a secret code the average person can't crack. The truth is that living trusts, when "revocable" (changeable during your lifetime), don't add unnecessary layers for most people. They are meant to be adjusted as life changes. The real hurdle isn't complexity, but occasionally the lack of the right guidance.

Take the case of a single homeowner worried about paying thousands in legal costs. After talking to a fee-only estate planning attorney, she learned that setting up a basic revocable living trust can often cost about the same as a typical will plus advanced directives—only with fewer costs down the line for probate. Many states now allow guidance for filling out "pour-over" wills (which work with your trust) in simple, accessible ways. Ongoing fees are often minor. Some online horror stories make costs seem higher, but they often involve very complicated family or tax situations.

Living Trusts Mean Giving Up Control Over Assets

Hesitation often appears when the topic turns to **control**. Many people imagine that placing their bank accounts or homes into a trust means surrendering ownership or needing permission for every change. This confusion usually stems from mixing up **revocable** and **irrevocable** trusts. A **revocable living trust** allows its creator—known as the **grantor**—to change or dissolve the trust at any time, as long as they are alive and mentally capable. Owning assets "in trust" does not mean giving up control. If you name yourself as **trustee**, you can continue managing and spending those assets just as you always have.

One man in his early fifties recalled how a neighbor warned him he'd "never be able to sell" his truck once it was in a trust. Concerned, he checked with his estate adviser, who clarified that as trustee, he retained full authority to buy, sell, trade, or gift anything within the trust while he was alive. The paperwork might show the trust's name on the title, but the decision-making power remained entirely his. Unless a trust is specifically designed to limit access—a rare choice for living trusts—the creator stays firmly in control.

Living Trusts Replace the Need for a Will—Or Other Myths About Effectiveness

Some sources blur the relationship between wills and trusts, making people think one cancels the other. In fact, both tools can work together. A living trust organizes the main assets you transfer into it. Anything you own that's not titled in the trust may still pass under your will. That's why many people have a simple "pour-over" will to catch anything left outside the trust and move it over at death.

Confusion also arises when people see headlines about trust disputes. These stories often involve problems outside the trust itself: poor updates, inadequate communication, or deliberate fraud. Careful record-keeping and periodic review minimize these issues. Reliable information often comes from state bar associations, certified planning attorneys, or the official court resources. Relying on viral online stories or unverified social media posts can lead to stress or missteps.

Spotting Reliable Guidance and Moving Forward

Checking credentials and looking for plain, clear language in legal explanations helps filter out noise. Official state or national bar groups' resources, books by neutral professionals, and direct communication with known lawyers or planners beat rumor every time. Feeling empowered starts with knowing where myths come from, how living trusts really work, and how to match your plan to your needs. With time spent on solid information, you can plan with added confidence and less confusion, ready to use tools that fit your life, not someone else's story.

Bringing It All Together

Now that you understand the basics of living trusts—their purpose, key terms, and how they differ from wills—you are better equipped to make informed decisions that protect your assets and ease the burden on your loved ones. By choosing a living trust, you can ensure privacy, avoid lengthy probate delays, and maintain control over how and when your property is shared. With clear knowledge removing common fears and misconceptions, you can confidently explore the next steps in estate planning, creating a plan that fits your unique needs and offers peace of mind for you and your family's future.

CHAPTER 2

IS A LIVING TRUST RIGHT FOR YOU?

Have you ever wondered how to protect your family's future without leaving them caught in long, expensive court battles? What if your property is spread across multiple states, or you own a small business that needs steady management when you're no longer able to lead it? Many people wrestle with these questions quietly, unsure which tools truly fit their situation. Some worry that the legal documents will be too complicated; others hesitate to plan at all, uncertain whether their wishes will be honored exactly as they intend.

These concerns are both common and deeply human. They encapsulate the essence of estate planning—ensuring the well-being of those you cherish after your passing. This chapter invites you to explore whether a **living trust** might be the right solution for your needs, helping you understand how it compares to other options and whether it offers the control, privacy, and peace of mind you're looking for.

Who Benefits from a Living Trust: Typical and Special Circumstances

Deciding who benefits most from a living trust begins with looking at property owners. Homeowners and anyone with real estate often face long, expensive probate if they only have a will. A living trust removes real property from probate, letting it pass directly to heirs. For instance, if a couple owns a home together, placing the property in a living trust lets the surviving partner or children take ownership with little delay or court cost. This direct route becomes even more valuable when someone holds property in multiple states, since each location typically requires its own probate case. With a living trust, these assets are managed under a single plan, saving time and legal fees.

Owning other assets, such as investment accounts, family businesses, or second homes, can also motivate people to set up a living trust. Someone running a small business, for example, risks interruption for employees and clients if they die without clear instructions for who takes over. By naming a successor trustee in the trust, a business owner ensures continued management or simple closure. This could mean naming an adult child to run the shop, dividing business shares among siblings, or selling the business and splitting profits. No matter the plan, the living trust keeps decisions private and immediate, out of the probate court.

For parents and grandparents—especially those raising minor children or caring for dependents with disabilities—a **living trust** offers far greater control than a will. Consider a single parent with two children under 18. If they leave only a will, the court will manage any inheritance for the minors under strict rules with limited investment flexibility. When the children turn 18, they receive the full amount at once, even if the parent wanted the funds to support them gradually through college or other milestones. A living trust allows the parent to schedule distributions over time, fund education and healthcare, and appoint a trusted person to manage assets until the children are ready. For families with a child who has special needs, a trust can also prevent direct inheritance that might jeopardize eligibility for government assistance—while ensuring lifelong financial support.

Blended families and those experiencing remarriage often benefit from the extra clarity and protection a trust provides. Imagine someone with children from a first marriage and a current spouse. Depending solely on a will could lead to conflict over who inherits the family home or personal belongings. A living trust can separate inheritances clearly—for example, granting the current spouse use of the home for life while reserving ownership for the children later. This structure helps prevent disputes and reduces the likelihood of costly court battles.

People planning for **declining health**—their own or a loved one's—also gain from the flexibility of a living trust. If the trust creator becomes ill or incapacitated, a named **successor trustee** can immediately take over financial management without court involvement. Bills continue to be paid, investments maintained, and dependents cared for, eliminating the need for guardianship or conservatorship proceedings. For retirees, this layer of assurance becomes especially valuable.

Finally, **privacy** is one of the strongest reasons people choose a living trust. Wills must pass through probate, becoming part of the public record—meaning banks, neighbors, or even distant relatives can see your assets and who receives them. A living trust, by contrast, remains private. Only trustees and beneficiaries know its details, protecting both family privacy and heirs from unwanted attention or pressure.

Living trusts also help people with assets in more than one state by solving the challenge of multiple probate courts. A retiree owning vacation property in another state can include it in the trust, so heirs avoid having to hire lawyers in both locations. The trust centralizes all property, making the process seamless and coordinated.

Sometimes, family members need protection from their own circumstances. A parent may want to protect an adult child's inheritance from creditors, divorce settlements, or unwise spending. With a living trust, the trustee can hold funds until the child reaches a certain age or meets other conditions, protecting assets that a simple will might leave vulnerable.

Still, living trusts are not a catch-all. Some people with very simple assets or without concerns about minors or real estate may find a will that covers their needs. Wills remain vital for choosing guardians for minor children, naming funeral wishes, or passing on certain sentimental items. Legal experts often recommend integrating both tools—a living trust to avoid probate and manage assets, and a will to handle any property not included in the trust and to name guardians for young children. Each person's situation shapes the right estate plan, and using both gives flexible options and peace of mind for families with evolving needs.

The Continuing Role of Wills in Estate Planning

Advantages of a living trust often stand out: privacy, probate avoidance, and greater control over asset distribution. Yet property owners can overlook that a trust, even one tailored to their needs, cannot fully replace a will. A will serves as a critical safety net for family members, personal wishes, and unaddressed issues in the estate plan.

A will is a legal document that spells out a person's wishes for their property and responsibilities after death. Unlike a living trust, which can transfer ownership of certain assets to named beneficiaries while the grantor is still alive, a will becomes effective only at death and covers a larger set of personal matters. A trust mainly deals with assets held within it, but a will has a wider reach, directing the distribution of property not titled or transferred to the trust and handling family and personal concerns a trust just cannot.

Unique Functions Served by a Will

Some roles are unique to a will. One of the most vital is the appointment of a guardian for minor children. A trust cannot make guardianship designations; only a will lets parents choose who will raise their children if both are gone. Without this direction, state courts will decide, which may not match a parent's wishes.

A will also deals with personal property not formally assigned to the trust. This might mean favorite pieces of jewelry, family heirlooms, cars, artwork, or even sentimental gifts promised but not documented elsewhere. If a person acquires new property and forgets to retitle it into the trust, the will captures those items and clarifies where they go.

Real-World Scenarios Where a Will Remains Indispensable

- **Guardianship Needs**: A single parent with a living trust still needs a will to state who will care for children in their absence. If no will exists, guardianship decisions fall to the courts, often based on family hierarchy or local law rather than personal preference.
- **Unfunded Property**: Imagine a homeowner who refinances and retitles the house back into personal ownership but passes away before transferring it back into the trust. The house falls outside the trust—only a will can direct its distribution.
- **Personal Gifts**: Someone collects rare stamps and stores them in a safe deposit box. They never move the collection into the trust. The will details who inherits the stamps, making sure this personal wish is honored.
- **Recently Acquired Assets**: If an individual receives a car inheritance close to death, there may not be time to transfer it into the trust. The will steps in as the safety net for such assets.

The Role and Importance of a Pour-Over Will

The pour-over will is a practical solution for those who have a living trust. This special type of will acts like a catch-all, stating that any items or property not placed into the trust during life should be transferred ("poured over") into the trust at death. Assets outside the trust still go through probate, but they ultimately end up managed as intended within the trust's framework. A pour-over will is vital because no matter how careful someone is, there is often something left out.

Action Steps for Integrating a Will and Living Trust

Reviewing all assets is crucial. Start by listing everything owned—real estate, vehicles, investment accounts, personal items. Check each item's title and beneficiary designation. For each asset, decide: should it go into the trust, pass through a beneficiary form, or remain outside and be covered by the will? Retitle real estate, financial accounts, and other major assets into the trust as needed. Double-check that new assets are handled in a timely manner.

Keep both documents—the will and the trust—up to date. Major life changes like births, deaths, marriages, and divorces call for immediate review. Update guardianship choices for children, add new property to the trust, and modify bequests for personal items in the will as relationships and circumstances evolve.

Consulting with an estate planning professional can prevent costly mistakes, such as overlapping or conflicting terms between documents. Many assume a living trust automatically replaces the need for a will, but this is not true. A will remains necessary for everything that trust cannot reach.

Maximizing the Power of Both Tools

A trust directs major assets; a will gives instructions for remaining wishes and property. Both work together to cover gaps and avoid mistakes. Careful coordination of asset titles, beneficiary forms, and document terms ensures smooth handling of property and personal matters. Regular review of assets, attention to personal wishes, and professional guidance when needed combine to create a working, flexible plan.

As people's lives change, the living trust's flexibility and revocable nature can adapt to new family or property needs. This means readers can remain confident that their estate plan will continue to serve their goals, and they will be ready to learn more about how revocable living trusts keep pace with life's changes.

Flexibility of Revocable Living Trusts

Wills usually outline what happens after you die, but they don't always allow for quick or easy adjustments while you're alive. Life keeps moving—families grow, priorities shift, and circumstances change—and that's where the flexibility of a **revocable living trust** truly stands out. A revocable living trust is a legal arrangement in which you, as the trust maker (or **grantor**), place your assets—homes, savings, investments, or even a small business—into a trust that you control completely as long as you remain mentally capable. You decide who receives what, when, and under what conditions, while keeping the power to revise your plan whenever life takes a new direction.

A revocable living trust grows and adapts with you. If your family changes—a new grandchild is born, a child marries, loved ones relocate, or relationships evolve—the trust adjusts easily. You might sell a house, start a business, or acquire new investments over the years. At these pivotal moments, the trust does not confine you or compel you to begin anew. Instead, you can add or remove beneficiaries, update asset lists, or even change your successor trustee with minimal effort.

There are two main ways to update your trust: **amendments** and **restatements.** An **amendment** works like an update to a contract—you create a short document specifying what you want to change, sign it, and attach it to your existing trust. It's ideal for smaller updates, such as adding a new beneficiary after a marriage or birth. For example, if your daughter welcomes a baby, you can simply amend the trust to include your new grandchild as a beneficiary. Or, if you decide to give a family heirloom to someone different, a quick amendment updates your wishes instantly.

A **restatement** is broader in scope. When you want to make multiple changes or reorganize your trust's language, you can restate the entire document while keeping the same name and date. This avoids confusion later and keeps titles and account ownership intact. You (and your co-trustee, if applicable) sign the restatement and store it with your existing paperwork. For major life changes—such as relocating to a new state, selling significant property, or restructuring your estate after a divorce—a restatement provides a fresh start without having to dissolve the old trust or re-title every asset.

People often worry that these updates require long meetings or big lawyer bills. In reality, as long as you're mentally capable, changes are usually straightforward—sometimes even a single page. Many families handle simple amendments themselves using templates, or they pay for a single session with a professional. If your trust gets complex or holds lots of property, an estate planner can guide you, but the process remains much easier and more private than redoing a will or creating an irrevocable trust.

Picture a family-owned business that expands after a decade. The parents want to include their two adult children and a son-in-law as beneficiaries while putting guidelines on selling shares. With a revocable trust, they amend the document to add the new family members and set the instructions without re-signing all the business property. Or, think about a blended family, newly married with stepchildren on both sides. Updating the trust means including everyone important, adjusting amounts left to each person, and making sure parent and stepparent wishes are honored. There's no need to start over from scratch or risk missing someone.

Homeowners sometimes choose to downsize in retirement, selling a long-time house and moving closer to family. The new property and any profits slide directly into the trust by updating the asset listing—no need to make a new will or start a new trust. The same goes for adding new bank accounts or selling off investments; the changes are managed by updating your trust schedule and, when needed, a simple amendment.

Flexibility also means full control over the assets in the trust. The trust maker can invest, buy or sell property, add or remove beneficiaries, attach new conditions, and even revoke (officially cancel) the trust at any time. Nothing is locked until death or incapacity, providing strong reassurance that your wishes stay current with your life. If your best friend, chosen as a future trustee, moves abroad and can't help, you swap in someone local with an amendment.

Comparing estate planning options makes this clear:

- **Revocable living trust:** Can be changed or cancelled by maker at any time while alive and capable; assets added or removed easily; beneficiaries updated as life shifts.
- **Wills:** Must be revised or replaced each time you want changes. Final and public at death, more formal.
- **Irrevocable trusts:** Cannot be adapted after setup except in rare cases—no way to change beneficiaries or reclaim assets.

Flexibility enables you to respond to joys, setbacks, and surprises with confidence. Your plan keeps pace with your family, assets, and wishes. This makes a revocable living trust a strong comfort for anyone hoping estate planning will serve not only today's needs but the ones still to come.

Bringing It All Together

Now that you understand how a living trust can protect your assets, provide for loved ones, and adapt to life's changes, you are better equipped to decide if it fits your unique estate planning needs. By carefully considering who benefits, acknowledging the ongoing importance of a will, and embracing the flexibility of revocable trusts, you can create a comprehensive plan that avoids probate, safeguards privacy, and offers peace of mind. As your family grows and circumstances evolve, this knowledge empowers you to take practical steps—whether updating documents or seeking professional advice—so your estate plan remains strong, clear, and tailored to secure your legacy well into the future.

CHAPTER 3
PLANNING YOUR TRUST—WHAT TO DECIDE BEFORE YOU WRITE IT

Have you ever paused to consider what truly needs to be decided before creating a trust? How do you ensure every important detail is covered so your wishes are clear and your loved ones are protected? Many people begin drafting a trust without fully understanding the key choices involved, which can lead to confusion, delays, or unintended consequences. Before putting pen to paper, essential decisions about what property to include, who will manage it, who benefits from it, and how distributions should work must be thoughtfully made. This chapter will guide you through those crucial considerations, helping you build a solid foundation for your trust planning that avoids common pitfalls and sets the stage for a smooth transfer of your assets.

Assessing and Listing Your Assets for the Trust

Building a trust begins with a clear, detailed list of everything a person owns that might fit within a trust. Recognizing the necessity of this list can make what looks overwhelming feel manageable. Assets, in this context, are anything of value you have legal claim to—property, money, shares, retirement funds, business interests, personal valuables, and even digital assets like intellectual property and royalties. For trust planning, assets can be grouped into two categories: probate and non-probate property. Probate property includes assets that would, without a trust, pass through a court-supervised estate process after death—things owned solely in your name with no specific beneficiary. Non-probate property passes directly to another person or entity upon your death, such as accounts or insurance policies with named beneficiaries, or property held jointly with right of survivorship.

Both asset types deserve careful review, as trusts often cover both, though the method may differ. Real estate is usually the most valuable asset for many. This covers not only a person's primary residence but also vacation homes, rental properties, or land. Cash and bank accounts—checking, savings, and certificates of deposit—are straightforward. Investments and retirement accounts are vital but sometimes tricky. Standard brokerage accounts can often be retitled in the name of a trust, but tax-advantaged retirement accounts like IRAs or 401(k)s usually cannot have ownership transferred while the original owner is alive. Life insurance policies can list a trust as beneficiary, allowing proceeds to pass to the trust, though policies themselves typically do not transfer.

Other investment assets, like stocks, bonds, mutual funds, annuities, and health savings accounts, should also be considered. Business ownership adds another layer. Sole proprietorships, shares in a family company, or interests in partnerships or LLCs might be placed into a trust, but partnership or corporate agreements sometimes limit transfers; it's wise to review legal documents before listing these.

Personal property, such as vehicles, boats, and even airplanes, might also be included, depending on value and state law. Significant personal items often carry more meaning than monetary worth: jewelry, collections, art, antiques, or family heirlooms can go into a trust for clear transfer and to avoid disputes. Intellectual property—copyrights, patents, trademarks, and royalties—should be inventoried and may be placed in a trust, so long as ownership is clear.

Here's an example of a diverse asset inventory:

- Primary residence (123 Oak Lane)
- Vacation home (Lakeview Cabin)
- Checking account at Neighborhood Bank
- Brokerage account with mutual funds and bonds
- IRA (cannot transfer ownership to trust, but can list trust as beneficiary)
- Shares in Johnson Family LLC
- 2019 Toyota Camry
- Valuable watch collection
- Life insurance policy (XYZ Life Insurers)
- Copyrights from published books
- Art and rare coin collections

Identifying these assets is only the beginning. A practical method involves moving step-by-step. First, walk room by room in each property, making a list of all real estate owned, then noting valuable personal items found in each space. This includes garages, safety deposit boxes, attics, and storage units. Next, gather financial documents: bank account statements, investment summaries, retirement plan details, insurance policies, business documents, deeds, and titles. Review digital records as well, like online payment accounts or cryptocurrency holdings.

Gather documents that prove ownership—titles, deeds, share certificates, beneficiary statements, contracts, and appraisals. Write the current estimated value beside each item on your list. You don't need formal appraisals unless values are unclear; a reasonable market estimate is sufficient for planning. Because life changes—marriage, divorce, the birth of a child, or acquiring or selling assets—update this list during major milestones so it remains accurate and reliable.

Some assets involve **joint ownership** or **named beneficiaries.** For example, property owned with a spouse or business partner may pass automatically outside of probate, unless the co-owner has already passed away. Accounts with "transfer on death" (TOD) or "payable on death" (POD) designations, as well as insurance policies or retirement plans listing specific beneficiaries, may not need to be included in a trust unless you want different instructions or additional control. In these cases, confirm directly with each financial institution how those accounts will transfer.

When ownership details are uncertain—or when describing a business interest—it's wise to consult a lawyer or tax professional. However, compiling your list and gathering documentation can happen first. Once your asset inventory is complete, later steps in trust planning become far simpler. The next step—**choosing your trustee and backup**—naturally follows once you have a clear picture of your estate. In the next section, we'll explore how to select the people or institutions best equipped to carry out your wishes with care and precision.

Appointing Trustees and Identifying Beneficiaries

Choosing who will manage your trust is the next clear step after you have listed your assets. Your chosen trustee will oversee the meticulous execution of your instructions. A trustee's job reaches beyond simply handing out property—this is someone who must handle money, pay bills, settle debts, file tax forms, and keep records that might later be needed by both the trust's beneficiaries and outside organizations like the IRS. Organization and reliability matter a lot. If someone is regularly late with their own bills or sometimes lets details slip, overseeing a trust might not fit them. It also helps if the person stays clear of family arguments and can let go of their own opinions and follow written instructions.

What Makes a Strong Trustee

You can pick a family member, a close friend, or a professional such as a trust company, accountant, or lawyer. Many people think of their oldest child, but this approach does not fit all families. Ask yourself questions: Does this person handle stress well? Can they be fair if children or siblings disagree? If you sense rivalry or any history of putting one person's needs above another, think twice. Also consider work and life circumstances—does your possible trustee have time to do the job well?

Sometimes, naming a friend or someone outside your immediate family works better. A neutral party can keep things straightforward when emotions run high. For bigger trusts, or when property is spread between states, a professional trustee may help avoid costly mistakes. Professional trustees charge fees, but reliability is their business. But friends or family may know your needs better than a pro, and they might do it for free.

Real-World Example

Suppose Jim picks his eldest daughter, Sandra, because she is the oldest and lives nearby. Sandra tries, but paperwork piles up, and when her brother asks about the trust, she leaves his requests unanswered. Disagreements get worse. In another family, Alice chooses her sister-in-law, who acts calmly and lets everyone see the records. The process finishes without drama, and all instructions get carried out. Picking a trustee who is steady and clear-headed helps protect against both mistakes and hurt feelings.

Why You Need a Successor Trustee

Even the best trustee can become unwilling or unable to serve because of illness, work, or death. A successor trustee steps in if the first trustee can't continue. Without a backup, your trust might need a court to appoint someone, which can take time and open old wounds. Clearly listing a successor helps everything stay on track and keeps your wishes at the center of every step.

Picking Your Beneficiaries—and Their Backups

A primary beneficiary is your first choice—this is the person or charity meant to receive your assets. A backup (sometimes called "contingent beneficiary") will inherit only if the primary beneficiary can't, because of death or any other reason.

Steps for Naming Beneficiaries

1. Write down can't because a group you want to inherit, using full names.
2. Choose whether to name people individually or by group, such as "my children, in equal shares."
3. If you name a child who is a minor, think about naming a guardian to manage their share.
4. For blended families, be clear—if you mean biological children only or want stepchildren included, write that down.
5. For charities or organizations, use their full legal names to avoid confusion.

Scenario: You name your sister as the primary beneficiary, but if she passes away before you, you want her daughter to inherit. You can write, "to my sister, Jane Smith," or, if she is not living, "to her daughter, Emily Smith." This step makes sure the property doesn't go somewhere you never intended.

Managing Complicated Family Situations

Families change over the years. Divorces, remarriages, estrangement, or new grandchildren call for careful thinking. In these cases, spelling out exactly who gets what helps avoid hurt and legal fights. For blended or uncertain relationships, some write, "to my spouse and all children born to or legally adopted by me, in equal shares." If you want to exclude someone, it should be direct and unmistakable within the trust. If you want an estranged child to inherit, but only under certain conditions, a clear description helps.

Reviewing your beneficiary choices regularly is wise, especially after big changes like marriage, divorce, or birth of a grandchild. Your trust remains effective only if your choices match your real wishes as life carries on.

Smooth trustee appointments and carefully listed beneficiaries lay the groundwork for organized asset transfer. Who you name and how you define their shares mean your values will shape what happens to everything you leave behind. Deciding how, when, and under what terms those assets get divided comes next.

Determining Asset Distribution Plans

Deciding how and when to distribute assets is about making your intentions clear for the people you trust. The roles you assign—whether a thoughtful individual as your trustee or diligent alternates to step in if needed—affect the path your trust will follow and the lives of your beneficiaries. Each choice about who receives assets and when can influence how your family interacts for years to come.

Common ways to distribute trust assets

Several approaches stand out when deciding how assets should reach your beneficiaries. Outright distribution gives them everything at once, usually after your death or another fixed event. This way works well for mature adults with responsible spending habits or for relatively small estates where further oversight seems unnecessary. It offers speed and simplicity. Nevertheless, giving a large sum to a young or inexperienced heir can bring risks of poor decisions, temptation for creditors, or challenges during divorce settlements.

Staggered distributions divide the payout into pieces delivered over time or at set milestones. For instance:

- One-third at age 25
- Half the remainder at 30
- Balance at 35

This method can encourage long-term financial maturity, since beneficiaries have time to learn from earlier experiences. It also comforts parents or grandparents who worry about reckless spending with a sudden windfall. Drawbacks include added administrative work for your trustee and possible frustrations for beneficiaries who want or need more flexibility.

Conditional distributions tie payouts to specific achievements or life events. Some conditions people use include:

- Graduation from college
- Marriage
- Maintaining employment
- Completing addiction treatment

A trust might say, "Distribute up to $20,000 upon proof of a bachelor's degree," or "Release funds for the down payment of a first home." These conditions can motivate your beneficiaries, but they work best when requirements are simple to prove. Overly complex or vague wishes can leave your trustee stuck in the middle if someone disagrees about whether a condition was met.

Pros and cons at a glance

- **Outright:** Quick, no red tape, but risk of careless spending
- **Staggered: It promotes responsibility and safeguards youth, but requires longer oversight.**
- **Conditional:** Encourages goals and personal growth, but can frustrate or delay access

Considering timing and its impact

The moment a beneficiary receives their share shapes what they do with it. Immediate access brings instant freedom, yet some people prefer to delay distributions. They do this to help protect minors or shield assets from creditors, lawsuits, or even divorce settlements. A trust can set twenty-one, twenty-five, or thirty as the magic ages for large gifts, reducing a spendthrift risk.

Some families use the trust to pay only for educational or medical costs while someone is a minor, then open the rest of the funds after age thirty. Grandparents may wish to see grandchildren's college costs covered and then have any unspent funds released as young adults reach financial independence.

Delays can cause tension if someone feels entitled to "their" money, so clear communication within the trust is helpful. Some people include a note explaining choices, like "I want each heir to fully complete college before receiving the entire gift," so wishes feel rooted in care, not control.

Writing clear, precise instructions

Trustees need directions that leave no room for guessing. Saying "divide equally between my children" works better than "as you see fit," which risks confusion and arguments. Phrasing like "pay each grandchild $10,000 for tuition to an accredited college" makes intentions direct and avoids gaps.

Families with children from more than one marriage may need extra clarity: "After selling the home, give fifty percent of the proceeds to my daughter, Jane, and twenty-five percent each to my sons, Rick and Thomas." Anticipate what questions might come up, such as, "Does someone qualify as a beneficiary if adopted after your death?" If a child dies first, can their share be passed on to their own children? A little extra detail in your writing lets trustees act with confidence and prevents misunderstandings.

Balancing control with flexibility

Desiring order shouldn't block smart decisions in emergencies. A trust can let your trustee use skills and judgment you trusted them for in the first place. You might write, "You may make early distributions for severe medical needs or approved emergencies as you deem prudent." By drawing clear boundaries—like capping extra payouts or limiting them to family, not creditors—you give both direction and breathing room.

Some families limit trustee discretion to prevent favoritism, while others want their trustee to help beneficiaries with unforeseen crises. Outlining these wishes gives your trustee confidence to act and keeps everything fair. Simple steps, real examples, and your personal touch combine to create strong instructions that reflect what you value most.

Bringing It All Together

Thoughtful planning of your assets, trustees, beneficiaries, and distribution methods forms the foundation of a successful trust that honors your wishes and protects your family's future. By carefully assessing what you own and choosing reliable people to manage and receive those assets, you can prevent confusion, delays, and disputes later on. Clear instructions about how and when assets will be shared give your trustee the confidence to act wisely while providing your beneficiaries with security and fairness. Now that you have a solid inventory and understand the key decisions ahead, you are ready to move forward with drafting your trust, turning your plans into a clear, actionable document that brings lasting peace of mind.

CHAPTER 4
CREATING THE TRUST—STEP-BY-STEP WITHOUT A LAWYER

"I just don't know where to start," Maria whispered, staring at the blank screen before her. The forms, the legal words, the instructions—it all felt like a tangled mess that could easily lead to mistakes. She wanted to create a trust for her children, something clear and solid, but without paying sky-high lawyer fees. Meanwhile, across town, Steve scanned a free template he had found online. It seemed simple enough, but as he filled in the blanks, questions about his blended family's needs nagged at him. Was this really enough to protect everything? Could he get it done on his own without missing something important?

These moments are familiar for many who decide to take control of their estate plans without an attorney. The path isn't always obvious, and the choices about how to draft your trust can feel overwhelming. Finding the right approach means balancing ease, cost, and confidence while avoiding common errors that could undo months or years of effort. Yet with clear steps and practical tools, setting up a trust independently is not only possible—it can offer peace of mind knowing your wishes are written down and ready to stand up in court if needed.

Behind the hesitation and uncertainty lies a straightforward process broken into manageable parts. Each decision—from selecting your drafting method to signing the final document—shapes how well your trust will serve you and those you care about. This chapter guides you through those decisions and provides the roadmap to navigate the complexities calmly, helping you build a legally sound trust without needing a lawyer at every turn.

Choosing Your Drafting Method and Avoiding Common Pitfalls

Understanding how to start creating a trust without an attorney means choosing a method that lines up with your confidence, your family's needs, and your level of comfort filling out legal documents. You have three proven ways to draft your trust on your own: DIY software, packaged trust kits, and downloadable templates. Each offers a different mix of support, cost, and flexibility.

DIY trust software offers a guided, step-by-step experience on your computer or tablet. These programs function like wizards: they ask about your family, property, and wishes, then generate a trust by filling in the necessary legal language. If you encounter a difficult question, many include help menus or chat support. Most also stay updated with current state laws and automatically check for missing information or common errors before you print and sign. You typically pay a one-time fee of about **$60–$120**. This approach works best for those who want guided support, have straightforward family needs (such as leaving everything evenly to children or a spouse), and want extra assurance that state requirements are met. The main drawback comes with complex situations—blended families, special needs dependents, or unusual assets—where the software may lack flexibility or limit custom instructions.

Printed or digital trust kits provide another user-friendly path. These include explanations, glossaries, and step-by-step checklists for completing the documents yourself. The trust form is either pre-printed or downloadable, and you fill in the blanks by hand or using a word processor. Kits generally cost **$25–$60** and are easy to find online or in major bookstores. They suit people who prefer a tangible guide and like seeing everything laid out on paper. The included examples help beginners get started confidently. However, kits rarely include ongoing updates, meaning their advice may not reflect recent state law changes. Their checklists also catch only basic mistakes, offering less protection against contradictions or state-specific signature rules.

Downloadable or fill-in-the-blank templates are the quickest and least expensive option. These are simple Word or PDF files with blank fields for your information. Some are free, while premium versions run about **$10–$30**. Templates offer total flexibility for those who already understand trust basics and want to customize every detail. However, because they lack glossaries or built-in guidance, there's a higher risk of missing key requirements or including wording that doesn't align with your state's laws. Templates work best for experienced DIYers—often those with legal or estate-planning knowledge—who are confident reviewing their own work.

Choosing the Right Fit: Two Example Scenarios

Maria is a single parent who owns a small home and wants everything to go equally to her two children. She feels nervous about missing a step, so she buys DIY trust software. The guided questions keep her on track, and the program double-checks her state's signature rules. The process feels safe, and Maria gets a printout ready for her to sign and notarize.

In contrast, Steve wants a trust for his blended family. He downloads a free template to save money. It doesn't cover stepchildren, and he forgets to include key property. Months later, he finds out that courts may not honor his wishes because the template language didn't match his family situation or property list. Steve's mistake shows that saving money upfront can cost you in clarity and enforceability.

Common Mistakes to Avoid

- Using generic language from a template that doesn't match your family or property

Not changing sections or leaving standard phrases can mean the courts have trouble understanding or following your wishes. Always update template text to reflect your own details. Read each section aloud to check if it really fits your plan.

- Forgetting state signature requirements

Some states need witnesses and notarization on the main trust or the property schedules. Missing these can mean your trust is not valid. To avoid this, check your state's rules and have all needed signatures and notarizations before storing the document.

- Not transferring property into the trust

Many people write their trust but forget to legally move their property titles, accounts, or deeds into the trust's name. If you don't, the trust remains empty. Gather a list of assets, use your trust's legal name, and follow up by changing deeds, titles, or account registrations as your bank or state requires.

Strong, clear instructions and a direct drafting method make the path to a successful trust easiest to follow. Taking control with the approach that fits your needs lays the groundwork for building a document that will protect your assets and honor your wishes in every detail. Trust creation works best when you have the right tools and a clear understanding of each step ahead.

Composing the Trust Document: Sample Language and Walkthrough

Choosing your drafting method—software, template, or kit—sets the stage for creating your trust document. After reviewing your options and picking the method that fits your comfort level, you can shift confidently into drafting. Your role now is to capture your wishes clearly, step by step, on paper. Each part of the document matters and deserves careful attention.

Trust Title and Introductory Clause

Start with a clear, simple title at the top, like "John Doe Revocable Living Trust." This lets anyone review your paperwork and immediately know what it is. Below the title, write an introductory sentence to establish the purpose and the trust's date. Use plain language such as

"This Trust Agreement is made on June 1, 2024, by John Doe of 123 Elm Street, City, State."

The introductory clause sets the foundation. It lists the trust creator (called the grantor or settlor), the original trustee, and the date the trust goes into effect. This opening creates a record and draws a line marking your assets as trust property from this point forward.

Declaration of Trust

A basic declaration states that you are transferring your property into the trust and naming yourself—often the grantor—as the initial trustee. Here's how to make this direct:

"I, John Doe, declare that I am creating this revocable living trust and serving as its initial trustee. I transfer ownership of the assets listed in this document to this trust."

If you want your spouse to serve as co-trustee, just name both of you: "John Doe and Jane Doe, as co-trustees."

Trustee and Successor Trustee Provisions

This part identifies who will carry out your wishes and manage the trust property now and after you cannot. Start by naming yourself or the primary trustee:

"The initial trustee shall be John Doe."

Then name at least one successor trustee, the person or people you trust to step in if needed. Add their contact information to avoid any confusion. Example:

"If I am unable or unwilling to serve as trustee, I nominate Jane Doe, 456 Maple Lane, City, State, as successor trustee."

Including successors makes sure the trust does not go in limbo if you become incapacitated or pass away. Spell out what counts as "unable" or "unwilling" if you wish—"unable" could mean medically unfit, for instance.

Property Schedule

A detailed list of each asset you want the trust to own keeps matters clear. In a section called "Schedule A" or similar, describe each asset. Group homes, accounts, and valuables separately. If you own real estate, describe each place in full:

- 123 Oak Street, City, State (Main Residence)
- 456 Pine Lane, City, State (Vacation Cabin)

For accounts or valuables, say:

- Savings account ending in 1234 at City Bank
- 2015 Honda CR-V, VIN: 1HGXXXXXXXXX
- Shares of ABC Corporation (50 shares), held at XYZ Brokerage

Be thorough—if you forget an asset, it might bypass the trust and go through probate. List each valuable item or property you want included, plain and simple.

Beneficiary Designations

List people or organizations who will receive assets. Use full names and relationships for individuals. For blended families, separate lines for each child or stepchild helps prevent disputes.

"Upon my death, I give all trust property in equal shares to my children: Emily Doe and Ryan Doe."

For charities:

"I give $10,000 to the Animal Shelter, EIN 12-3456789, located at 101 Pet Lane, City, State."

Ambiguity in beneficiary names leads to confusion or even legal battles, so write exactly who or what you mean.

Distribution Instructions

Clearly explain how you want your property divided. If you want a child to receive their share at a certain age, note it simply:

"Emily Doe will receive her share at age 25. Until then, the trustee may use the funds for her health and education at their discretion."

For unequal shares or special situations, spell out the percentages or conditions. Example for stepchildren:

"Ryan Doe receives 60%, and Lisa Smith (stepdaughter) receives 40%."

Review this part twice. If you write "children" but do not list names, a court might interpret your intent in a way you do not expect.

Final Thoughts on Drafting

Keep your language short, direct, and free from extra details. Courts and banks look for clarity—not fancy words or legal terms. Check each section for missing names, outdated addresses, or assets you may have overlooked. Avoid vague phrases like "as my family sees fit," which create uncertainty.

Once each part is in place, your document is almost ready to protect your wishes. Before it becomes official, you will need the right signatures, witnesses, and notarization. These last steps make the trust binding and recognized in law, ensuring your efforts carry full power for your loved ones.

Executing Your Trust: Witnessing and Notarizing Procedures

Holding a completed draft of your trust puts you in a strong position, but that document won't hold up in court—or at a bank—until it's properly executed. **Execution** means completing the legal steps that make your trust official, recognized, and protected against disputes. Skipping or mishandling even one step can lead to confusion, delays, or worse—your trust could be rejected, leaving your wishes and assets vulnerable. Banks, title companies, and courts honor only those trusts that meet strict legal standards. Following clear, predictable steps eliminates these risks and ensures your plan stands firm.

Each state sets its own **rules for witnesses**, but most require at least two. Witnesses serve as neutral observers who confirm you were of sound mind and acted voluntarily. The best witnesses are adults who are not mentioned anywhere in your trust. By law, beneficiaries—anyone set to inherit—cannot serve as witnesses. This prevents claims of undue influence or forged signatures. For example, if your daughter acts as a witness while also being a beneficiary, a court could later declare the trust invalid or require her to give up her share. Instead, choose witnesses such as a cousin, coworker, or friend who isn't named in the trust. Both must be present during the entire signing and willing to confirm your intent if ever questioned.

Here's how this plays out in real life: John creates a trust leaving everything to his friend Mike and asks Mike to serve as a witness. Years later, John's relatives challenge the trust in court. Because Mike signed as both witness and beneficiary, the judge invalidates the document—or at least removes Mike's inheritance. This simple mistake is entirely avoidable by choosing witnesses with no stake in the trust. Always double-check the document before anyone signs, and confirm that all witnesses are fully eligible.

Signing in the presence of witnesses follows a precise sequence. Use this standard procedure:

1. Gather everyone in the same room: you (the trust creator) and both witnesses.
2. Bring the unsigned, printed trust document and valid identification for yourself and your witnesses.
3. Verbally state your intention to sign the trust and have each witness do the same.
4. Sign your name in the designated spot as creator or "grantor."
5. Each witness, one after the other, signs below or beside your signature. They must see you sign, and you must see them sign. No one should leave the room until all signatures are complete.
6. If your state requires a notary at the same time, the notary should watch the entire process.

A signed trust gains even more strength once it's notarized. Notarization means an official "notary public" stamps your document after checking your identity. This proves the signatures are real and that you have not been pressured or impersonated. Notarization helps block fraud, and banks or courts often insist on it before they honor your instructions. Most adults can find a notary at their main bank branch, credit union, law office, UPS store, or through online notary platforms that offer video meetings for this purpose. Bring a government-issued ID, your unsigned trust, and your witnesses if your state or notary asks for them. Only sign in the notary's presence to ensure authenticity.

States share many basic rules, but a few add extra requirements such as more witnesses or using special paper. Before you sign, take five minutes to call your county clerk's office or visit your state's official court website. Ask if there are conditions for witnessing or notarizing a trust, such as a "self-proving affidavit" or extra signature pages. This short check prevents wasted effort and gives you peace of mind.

Keeping an eye out for common errors will keep your trust valid:

- Not having all parties present when signing
- Using a beneficiary or someone named in the trust as your witness
- Allowing witnesses to sign after you, or signing outside their presence
- Signing the trust before meeting the notary
- Failing to use a current, government-issued photo ID
- Missing a notary seal or incomplete notary section

Double-check the final document before you file it away. All required signatures, the notary's stamp, and dates must be clear and readable. Store the executed (officially signed and sealed) trust in a fireproof safe at home or a bank safe deposit box. Tell at least one family member or trusted friend where to find your trust if needed. An executed trust, correctly witnessed and notarized, is a legal shield—a clear set of directions that others must respect and follow.

Wrapping Up

Now that you understand the key methods and critical steps to create and execute a trust on your own, you are equipped to take control of your estate planning with confidence. By choosing the drafting approach that matches your needs and carefully following signature and notarization rules, you can build a clear, valid legal document that protects your assets and honors your wishes. With attention to detail and awareness of common pitfalls, your self-created trust will stand strong against challenges and avoid costly delays or confusion for your loved ones. This knowledge empowers you to move forward decisively, securing your family's financial future without relying on expensive legal help.

CHAPTER 5
FUNDING THE TRUST—MAKING IT LEGALLY EFFECTIVE

"Isn't signing the trust enough to protect everything?" a client once asked me after completing their estate plan. It's a common question, but one that often leads to serious problems if left unanswered. Creating a trust is an important first step in managing and passing on your assets, but it doesn't automatically control or protect what you own. Without properly funding the trust—making sure your property, accounts, and other valuables are legally transferred into it—the trust remains an empty shell.

This chapter explains why funding a trust is essential to make it effective, turning written instructions into real protection for your family and your legacy. You will learn the necessary actions to transfer ownership of various assets, from real estate to bank accounts and personal property, along with practical advice to avoid costly mistakes. By understanding these steps and following a clear, methodical process, you can ensure that your trust works as intended, sparing your loved ones unnecessary delays, expenses, and confusion.

Understanding What It Means to Fund a Trust and Why It's Essential

A trust, by itself, is just a document—a set of instructions written on paper and signed with the best intentions. Yet, this document does not actually do anything until it owns or controls property. "Funding" a trust means taking real steps to move ownership of your actual assets—like your house, savings, or investments—into the trust's name. This step turns the trust from words into a tool that can protect your wishes, avoid probate, and help your loved ones in the way you intend.

Many people believe their job is finished once they sign their revocable living trust, but the real work comes after. Unless you move your assets into the trust, it stays empty. Picture a safe: you can buy the world's most secure safe, set the perfect combination, and install it in your home, but if you never put anything inside, it cannot protect your valuables. A trust without assets works exactly the same way. You have crafted your safe, but you need to fill it for it to do its job.

Imagine a family where parents create a trust and appoint their two children as equal beneficiaries. They sign every form, pay for legal advice, and feel secure—yet they never change the title on their house, the ownership on their brokerage account, or the name on their savings account. When they pass away, these assets remain in their personal names. As a result, their accounts and property go through probate, a public and often slow court process, because the trust does not own anything. The court decides who receives the assets, and the process adds months or even years, along with costs and possible disputes among family members.

Now look at another family who creates a similar trust and follows through completely. The parents retitle their house and investment accounts to the trust. Their savings accounts and certificates of deposit are updated with the trust's name. They even check beneficiary designations for retirement accounts and life insurance, making sure they are consistent with their wishes. When these parents pass away, every asset "inside" the trust is not subject to probate. The trustee quickly and privately transfers everything to the children. There is no court drama, no public record, and no delay. The family avoids confusion and conflict. Their wishes are honored.

Assets that people often need to fund include real estate, bank accounts, investment accounts, stocks and bonds, and even valuable personal property. Each one requires a different process. For a house or condominium, this means signing and recording a new deed that lists the trust as the owner. For a checking or savings account, the bank changes the account title to the trust's name. Non-retirement investment accounts need the account name updated, while IRAs and life insurance might need you to change the beneficiary rather than transferring ownership outright.

Even smaller assets deserve attention. Jewelry, collectibles, or a family heirloom do not get titled formally. Instead, you list them on a written schedule or assignment to the trust. The key is that every type of asset needs its action—there is no automatic shortcut. Whenever you acquire new property—a new home, vehicle, or large bank deposit—consider how to bring it "under" your trust so it gets the same protection and passes directly to your loved ones.

Some skip or delay funding the trust because the process seems tedious. Yet, the true cost comes later: legal battles, lost privacy, and hard feelings among relatives all because the trust was never "filled" properly. Beneficiaries may face months of uncertainty, and your legacy can be put at risk. By funding your trust fully, you are thinking ahead for your family. You help them avoid court, skip paperwork headaches, save money, and keep details private.

A complete and well-funded trust gives you peace of mind. It eases stress and worry for your loved ones. It means that what you worked hard for gets where you want it to go, without strangers interfering or family members fighting. Now that you see why funding matters, you need to know exactly how to carry out these steps for each type of asset. The following guidance will walk you through the detailed process of making sure every item you own is protected by your trust.

Step-by-Step Guide: Transferring Property and Updating Ownership

A trust works only if the assets are actually placed under its control. Funding a trust means changing the legal ownership of property, accounts, and financial tools so that the trust, not any one individual, holds them. Without these clear transfers, a trust can be powerless, leaving assets outside and subject to delays or court procedures. Turning a signed trust into a real, working arrangement takes methodical steps, careful paperwork, and a close eye for details. Here's a guide to doing this for a range of common assets.

Transferring Real Estate into the Trust

Real estate rarely moves automatically into a trust; it must be retitled. This typically requires preparing a new deed that names the trustee as the property owner. A standard example: John and Mary Smith prepare a new deed for their house at 123 Oak Avenue that reads, "John and Mary Smith, Trustees of the Smith Family Trust dated 06/15/2023."

The steps are as follows:

1. Get a copy of the current deed and the property's legal description.
2. Prepare a new deed document, such as a quitclaim or warranty deed, listing the trust as the new owner.
3. Ensure the deed uses correct legal names and the full trust title and date.
4. Sign the deed before a notary.
5. Submit the signed deed to the local county recorder or land records office, where it's filed and made part of the public record.

Example Deed Language

> This QUITCLAIM DEED, made this ___ day of _____, 20__, by John Smith and Mary Smith, husband and wife, granting to John Smith and Mary Smith, Trustees of the Smith Family Trust dated 06/15/2023, the property described as follows: [legal description here].

Some states require extra steps, such as filing transfer tax documents or notifying the lender, especially if there's a mortgage. Always use the correct deed form for your state.

Funding Bank Accounts and Investments

Bank accounts, CDs, and brokerage accounts are often still in an individual's name until retitled. Banks and brokerages each have policies for trust transfers. Normally, you'll need:

- A copy of the trust document's title page and signature pages
- A certificate or abstract of trust (summarizes trust details for the bank)
- Valid identification for trustees

Write to your bank using language like:

"Please retitle savings account ending in 1234 to 'John Smith, Trustee, Smith Family Trust dated 06/15/2023.' Enclosed are copies of the trust and required identification."

Some banks may also have a trust account application to complete. For investment accounts, the custodial institution will walk you through transferring ownership or opening a new trust-titled account, moving assets from the old registration.

Using TOD and POD Designations

For accounts where retitling is complicated, consider a Transfer on Death (TOD) or Payable on Death (POD) designation. This tells the bank to pay the funds to your trust directly after death, instead of into the estate. Use designations like

"TOD – Smith Family Trust, dated 06/15/2023."

Retirement accounts, such as IRAs or 401(k)s, often work best by updating the beneficiary designation, not by changing ownership.

Updating Beneficiary and Ownership Forms

For life insurance, annuities, or retirement plans, ask for a beneficiary change form from the company. The proper way to fill this out to benefit the trust might be

"Primary Beneficiary: John Smith and Mary Smith, Trustees of the Smith Family Trust dated 06/15/2023."

Confirm the spelling, punctuation, and dates exactly match your trust documents. If the beneficiary language is wrong—wrong trust name, missing date, incomplete titles—the payout could end up going through probate or to the wrong party.

Funding Other Types of Property

Personal property like vehicles, valuable collections, or business ownership interests also needs attention. High-value items such as cars may require a new title application with the department of motor vehicles listing the trust as the owner.

For things without a title, such as jewelry, art, or household goods, use an "Assignment of Property to Trust" or a simple bill of sale.

Small Business Example

If the Smiths own 100 shares in Smith Family LLC, they sign an assignment document (often provided by the company) transferring their shares to the trust.

Documentation, Troubleshooting, and Follow-Up

After each asset is transferred, keep a copy of all deeds, assignments, account paperwork, and confirmation letters. Ask banks or officials for written proof showing the trust is now the owner or beneficiary.

File these records neatly. Not only does this make things easier for loved ones or future trustees, it's proof that your steps worked. Regularly check that accounts, property records, and insurance policies reflect the trust.

Looking Ahead

Careful tracking and following up protect your effort. Mistakes or incomplete paperwork can mean assets slip outside the trust. Knowing what can go wrong—and how to guard against it—will help ensure all the work pays off. Keeping these steps in order lays a strong path for the next phase: recognizing, fixing, and preventing funding mistakes before they cause bigger problems.

Avoiding the Biggest Mistake: Not Funding the Trust

Even after completing the paperwork and creating the trust, many people struggle with the next step—ensuring that the trust truly owns every asset. Creating a trust document by itself does almost nothing if your home, accounts, or life insurance still list you (or your spouse) as the owner. The trust remains empty until the assets are legally transferred. If property stays outside the trust, those assets are not protected or distributed according to your wishes. Instead, they may pass through probate—the public, court-supervised process that you tried to avoid by setting up a trust in the first place. This mistake can erase many of the benefits of estate planning. Even a well-written trust cannot control what it does not own.

Picture a typical situation: A person may spend months with a lawyer detailing their wishes for how a home and savings should benefit the family after their passing, but then they might forget to retitle the house or update the bank account ownership. Later, their children discover the house is still in the parent's name. The trust cannot direct what happens to it, so the court steps in. Probate brings extra costs and risks, delays, and turns private details into public records. Loved ones may have to sort things out through the courts, and assets might not go where you wanted.

Several common pitfalls trip up well-intended trust creators. Many believe that once the trust is drafted, it "automatically" takes charge of everything. That is not true. The trust only controls assets to which it actually holds title or is named as a beneficiary. Others assume assets will switch over by themselves when the trust creator passes away. In reality, without the proper forms and legal steps, accounts and property stay in your individual name, meaning the trust is skipped completely. Some people are unsure which kinds of property need to be moved—does the family home need to be retitled? What about a business, or an old savings account at a credit union? Retirement accounts and life insurance need a special step: updating the beneficiary to the trust or a trust beneficiary, which is often overlooked. One more hidden trap is refinancing a house after transferring it to the trust. Lenders sometimes require taking the property out of the trust to approve the loan, but after closing, the title must be transferred back in—an easy step to forget.

For each of these challenges, a plain strategy can keep mistakes from happening. Keeping an updated checklist of assets is the first move. Write down every account, policy, house, and valuable item, along with whose name is on the paperwork. Then, check each one: Does the title or deed show the trust as the owner or as the beneficiary? If not, ask the bank, broker, insurance company, or county office for their procedure. Never assume a transfer is finished until you have a copy of the new title or a written confirmation from the institution involved. For real estate, review the property deed and make sure it mentions the trust. For retirement accounts and life insurance, get written confirmation of beneficiary changes. This step takes some legwork but prevents trouble for your loved ones later.

Practical routines help keep everything on track. Do an "asset audit" at least once a year, or every time a big change happens, such as buying or selling a house, opening new bank accounts, or getting married, divorced, or having a child. If you move or refinance, review all real estate records again and make sure the trust is still the owner. New assets like cars, business shares, or valuable collectibles should also be considered. When in doubt, ask an institution directly if they see the trust listed as owner.

A simple repeatable plan sets you up for peace of mind:

1. Make and update a master checklist of every asset and account.
2. Audit the checklist after every big life event—new house, refinanced loan, new savings, new business.
3. Confirm the trust owns the asset or is listed as the beneficiary.
4. Keep copies of deeds, account statements, and beneficiary forms in a safe place.
5. Enlist a trusted helper or family member to know where these records are kept.

Sticking to this process gives loved ones the security you intend. By making sure assets are placed in the trust and checking regularly, you prevent court involvement and confusion. Decisions stay private, and your instructions are followed. For parents, homeowners, and business owners, this detailed approach is real protection for the people and projects that matter. Every step completed today spares your family from guesswork and courtrooms later on.

Final Thoughts

Now that you understand the critical importance of fully funding your trust, you can take confident, practical steps to protect your assets and ensure your wishes are honored without unnecessary delays or court interference. By methodically transferring each property, account, and valuable item into your trust and regularly reviewing these details, you create a smooth path for your loved ones to follow, sparing them from confusion, expense, and public scrutiny. This careful attention preserves your legacy and provides peace of mind today, knowing that your estate plan will work as intended when it matters most. With this knowledge, you are ready to move forward and complete the necessary actions that turn your trust from paper into real protection for your family's future.

CHAPTER 6

REAL ESTATE, PROPERTY, AND SPECIAL ASSETS

Have you ever faced the challenge of figuring out how to pass on your home, car, or treasured possessions without leaving your family tangled in legal red tape? Do questions about titles, taxes, and paperwork leave you feeling overwhelmed when planning for the future? Many people want to protect their property and ensure everything goes smoothly after they're gone, yet they aren't sure where to begin or what steps to take. What does it really mean to place real estate, vehicles, or business interests into a trust, and are there items that don't belong there at all? This chapter will guide you through these complex issues with clear explanations designed to help you take control of your assets while avoiding common pitfalls.

Transferring Real Estate and Income Properties into a Trust

Owning real estate brings major benefits, but things can get complicated when it's time to pass those assets to family. Transferring your home and other properties directly into your **trust** allows you to skip probate and give your beneficiaries a clear, hassle-free path to ownership. Instead of waiting months for the court to settle the estate, your loved ones can take over far more easily. You also reduce the risk of confusion or competing claims that sometimes arise when property titles aren't clearly defined after death.

The process starts with a bit of paperwork and a careful review of how your property is currently titled. Here's a typical example: a married couple wants to move their family home into their trust so it passes smoothly to their children. Their first step is to obtain a copy of the **current deed**—the legal document that confirms ownership. This can usually be obtained from the county recorder's office or the title company.

Next, they create a **new deed** that transfers ownership from "John and Susan Smith, husband and wife as joint tenants" to "John and Susan Smith, Trustees of the Smith Family Trust dated May 1, 2022." The legal description of the property must match exactly what appears on the original deed.

A **notary public** must witness the couple signing the new deed—this step is not optional. Counties will not accept or record a deed without notarized signatures. Once signed and notarized, the deed should be submitted for **recording** at the local county office. Some counties charge a small filing fee, but once the deed is recorded, the property officially becomes part of the trust. Once recorded, that office updates public records so everyone can see that the trust is the new owner. To confirm, the couple should request a certified copy after recording and keep it with their trust papers.

Sometimes state laws ask for specific forms or extra steps. In some places, a transfer-on-death deed is an option if you want to pass your home outside probate but are not ready for a full-blown trust. Some homeowners also need to file for property tax exemptions when retitling so these do not get lost in the shuffle. It's wise to contact your local tax office to see if your home needs to be re-approved for any tax breaks, like those for seniors or veterans.

If there's a mortgage on your property, things get a bit more technical. Many lenders include a "due-on-sale" clause in their loan papers, warning that the full balance can be required when ownership changes. Luckily, federal rules often let you move your main residence into a trust without triggering this clause—but it's best to call your lender before making any changes. Homeowners' insurance also needs to be alerted, adding the trust as an "additional insured." This keeps your coverage in place and avoids gaps after the transfer.

Rental homes, vacation cottages, or income properties bring an added layer of steps. When you move a rental house or condo into your trust, the title transfer process mirrors what you'd do for your main home. Start by preparing the new deed, signing and notarizing it, and recording it. On top of this, you must give notice to tenants. This letter explains that while ownership has shifted from your personal name to your trust, the day-to-day rent collection and property rules stay the same. If you use a property manager, inform them so they can update management agreements and payment instructions.

Keep leases and all trust paperwork together to avoid mix-ups. When you update your title, also update landlord/tenant agreements so rent checks go to the trust and rent income is reported under the trust's tax ID. Let's say you own a duplex. After recording the title transfer, you'd send both tenants a short letter with your new "landlord" name, provide the trust's contact information, and confirm any changes to how they pay rent. Update your bookkeeping by listing future property income and expenses under the trust. Make sure your successor trustee can find these records easily.

Numerous problems can lead to obstacles. Forgetting to notify mortgage or insurance companies, skipping notice to tenants, or misreporting rental income on your taxes may complicate things for you and your heirs. Each year, double-check that property taxes and insurance list the trust as the owner. When paperwork, trust names, and real estate descriptions match, you avoid confusion and help the next trustee manage things smoothly.

Checking trust-to-property alignment means that the trust correctly lists every address and property you own. If you inherit or sell property, update the information to keep your trust current. Each scenario—your main home, a family cabin, a rental apartment—comes with its own mix of forms and people to notify. Keeping clear records means your trust remains ready, and makes life easier for whoever steps in after you. Beyond real estate, you will need different steps for vehicles, collectibles, and business interests, each with their own best practices for transfer into your trust.

Including Vehicles, Valuables, Collectibles, and Business Interests

Many families begin their trust planning with real estate, but the same foundation applies when moving to assets like vehicles, valuables, and business interests. Trusts can hold many items beyond a home, creating a more complete safety net that covers a broad range of property and helps your loved ones avoid delays or complications down the road.

How to transfer vehicles

Adding a vehicle to a trust involves changing the legal title to list the trust as the owner. This is not limited to cars—boats, motorcycles, and even recreational vehicles fall into this category. Each type of vehicle comes with its own title and registration, and the steps for transfer generally include:

1. Contacting the relevant agency:

- Cars and motorcycles: Department of Motor Vehicles (DMV)
- Boats: State's boating commission or DMV
- RVs: DMV or specialty vehicle division

2. Completing the agency's title transfer form. Most forms require information about the trust, including its full legal name and sometimes the trust's date of creation.

3. Submitting a copy of the trust (sometimes only a certificate of trust) with the completed paperwork.

4. Paying any transfer fees required by the state agency.

5. Updating insurance to reflect the trust as the titled owner.

If you skip any of these steps, ownership remains with you as an individual, defeating the intent of making your vehicle part of your trust. For instance, when a couple decides to add their family minivan to their trust, they visit the DMV with their trust paperwork and fill out a transfer form, showing both their signatures if the vehicle is jointly owned. After paying the fees, the DMV issues a new title, and the couple then contacts their insurer to confirm the change in ownership on their policy. Boats and RVs follow a similar process, but some states require more involved documentation for specialty vehicles, so checking local requirements is always smart.

Practical points to keep in mind:

- Vehicles with active loans may need lender approval for a title transfer.
- For vehicles used in a business, special rules often apply and may make a trust transfer less suitable.

Including valuables and collectibles

Physical assets that do not have formal titles, such as jewelry, art, coin collections, sports cards, or antiques, require a different approach. These assets get included in a trust through a written assignment or detailed inventory. To provide a clear record, write up a list specifying each valuable item: describe it, note distinguishing features, and include photos or serial numbers. For high-value items like art, an appraisal gives your inventory more weight and supports insurance updates.

Updating insurance is vital when transferring valuables to a trust. Policies may need to match the trust as the legal owner, and values should reflect recent appraisals. Suppose a grandparent wishes to place her emerald necklace, gold watch, and a rare signed baseball card collection in her trust. She lists each item, attaches recent appraisals, and stores photographs with the inventory. Her insurance agent then updates the coverage so that loss or theft is covered, even though the trust is now the legal owner.

Without titles to transfer, the trust relies on your clear inventory. Large items, like antique furniture or sculptures, should get the same treatment: a written assignment, valuation, and updated insurance. Some items, such as collections, benefit from professional appraisals. This builds a stronger case for ownership and helps your trustee make decisions later.

Business interests: steps and cautions

Business interests, such as sole proprietorships, LLC shares, and small business stock, come with unique challenges. In most cases, you assign these assets to your trust through written transfer documents. Here's how the process typically unfolds:

1. Review ownership documents, like articles of incorporation, operating agreements, or stock certificates.
2. Check for transfer restrictions or notice requirements in those documents.
3. Complete an assignment of interest or stock transfer form, naming the trust as the new owner.
4. Update internal business records to reflect the trust's interest.
5. Talk with co-owners or partners, if any, to get their signed acknowledgement or consent, if required.

For example, a small business owner with an LLC reviews her operating agreement and finds a section that requires partner approval for transferring membership shares. After getting approval and signing a written assignment, she updates the LLC records and provides copies to the company's attorney and accountant.

Some states limit the ability to transfer certain types of business stock, or may require special approval from a regulatory body. Always look at the governing documents or speak with a business professional before making changes.

Risks and requirements

Failing to update paperwork, get new appraisals, or follow an agency's requirements can cause headaches later. A car not formally retitled to the trust remains outside the trust and may face probate. An art collection not inventoried might be hard to locate or divide. If a business transfer does not meet company guidelines, co-owners may contest it. Documents and valuations must stay current to guarantee the trust works as intended.

Also, not every asset belongs in a trust. Certain retirement accounts, items with active loans, and vehicles tied to a business may be handled better with other estate planning tools. Understanding these exceptions helps protect what really matters and set up the best plan for each item, leading into a look at assets that work differently or fall outside typical trust planning.

Assets Not Suitable for Trust Inclusion

Business interests, valuables, and collectibles often require special consideration when moving assets into a trust. Each piece has its own rules, paperwork needs, and sometimes, outside legal limits. Missteps in naming or transferring these assets can have lasting ripple effects on your taxes, your heirs, and your overall estate plan. This makes asset selection for your trust just as vital as asset protection. Picking what should stay out is as important as picking what goes in.

Retirement accounts such as 401(k)s and IRAs stand out among popular exclusions. Federal law treats these accounts as tax-protected vehicles tied directly to an individual. Moving a 401(k) or an IRA itself into a trust breaks this chain, causing the account to be "distributed" and taxed all at once. This wave of taxes could erase much of the value you've built over years of saving. A more effective way to fold retirement accounts into your plans is to name your trust as a beneficiary. For example, if your children are young, or if you need to protect a vulnerable adult, naming your trust allows you to direct how and when funds become available. But if the trust gets complicated, such as with multiple beneficiaries or payout rules, required minimum distributions (RMDs) can become tricky or force the account to empty faster than if a person were named. Review these beneficiary choices whenever family or tax situations shift. Double-check that all designations line up with your wider plan, and keep your account paperwork up to date.

Health Savings Accounts (HSAs) and Flexible Spending Accounts (FSAs) bring another wrinkle. Unlike checking accounts or stocks, the IRS only lets a living individual own an HSA or FSA. Ownership by a trust isn't allowed. If you want these funds to help heirs, check if you can name your trust as a final beneficiary. For HSAs, this may work if you want to send any leftover funds to your trust following your passing. Realistically, though, most people use these accounts to zero by the end of their life. Stay on top of rules with your account provider, and have a backup plan if you expect any unused funds—for example, by spending down eligible medical costs or carefully assigning account beneficiaries.

Life insurance policies take a different approach. You may wonder if you should transfer ownership to a trust or simply name your trust as beneficiary. Each path has different results. Naming the trust as the beneficiary means the payout will flow into the trust after you die, where rules you set will guide who gets it, when, and how. This is helpful if your beneficiaries are minor children or rely on special needs care, as it shields the payout from probate and outside claims. If you transfer policy ownership to a trust, though, the rules change; you must watch for gift tax triggers and the "three-year rule" (if you pass within three years of the transfer, the policy may still be counted as part of your taxable estate). For families with children, a life insurance trust can help manage money until those children reach an age you trust them with larger sums. Review your policy's owner and beneficiary lines regularly, and seek advice before making ownership changes.

Certain vehicles, boats, or trailers also deserve attention. These often come with titles and loans, each controlled by state law. Transferring a car or boat with an active loan into a trust may break the lender's rules and, in some cases, prompt them to call the loan due. Also, state laws may block trusts from owning certain vehicles entirely or call for extra paperwork. A practical workaround is the transfer-on-death (TOD) registration, available in many states. With a TOD, ownership passes to a named heir without probate, but you keep normal control while alive. In Arizona, for instance, a vehicle registered with a beneficiary can skip probate, just like payable-on-death accounts do for cash.

When it comes to foreign assets, placing a beach house in Spain or an account in Switzerland inside a US-based trust isn't always possible. Many countries have local ownership, reporting, or inheritance laws that block or complicate foreign property transfers into an American legal structure. Some people set up a separate trust in the country where the property sits or work with international estate planning professionals to create a coordinated solution.

Active business interests and professional licenses present some of the trickiest challenges. LLC memberships with operating agreements, some franchise licenses, or professional practice rights (like law or medicine) might prevent transferring to a trust unless you get approval from partners or regulators. Instead, business succession plans, buy-sell agreements, or naming beneficiaries within company paperwork can provide safe paths forward.

Finally, sentimental items like family photos or childhood drawings are not suited for a trust's asset list, as legal descriptions become unwieldy and open to dispute. Personal property memoranda, or "letters of instruction," attached to a will or trust, let you leave clear handling tips for such items. This gives heirs guidance while keeping your main documents focused and maintainable. Regularly reviewing and updating asset records and beneficiary designations helps avoid most headaches and ensures each asset gets the thoughtful planning it needs.

Final Thoughts

Now that you understand how to manage and transfer various assets into your trust—from real estate and vehicles to valuables and business interests—you're better equipped to protect your estate and simplify the process for your heirs. By carefully following the necessary steps, keeping records current, and knowing which assets should remain outside the trust, you can avoid costly delays and legal complications down the road. With this foundation in place, you can confidently move forward in creating a clear, effective plan that safeguards your family's financial future and ensures your wishes are honored with ease.

CHAPTER 7
TRUSTS, TAXES, AND SAVING BIG

More than half of American adults worry about the costs and complications their families might face after they pass away. Many assume that setting up a living trust will automatically reduce taxes or eliminate legal expenses, but the reality is more nuanced. Understanding how trusts work with taxes and legal processes is essential to making informed decisions that protect your assets and maximize savings for your heirs.

This chapter explains how revocable living trusts relate to income taxes, federal and state estate taxes, and legal fees associated with probate. You will learn why simply transferring assets into a trust does not change your tax responsibilities during your lifetime, how certain strategies can help minimize future tax burdens, and why careful organization and funding of a trust can save thousands in costly court fees. Clear guidance will help you navigate these topics confidently, ensuring your planning efforts translate into real benefits for you and your family.

Understanding Tax Basics and Estate Tax Implications for Living Trusts

Understanding how a **revocable living trust** affects taxes often clears up one of the biggest sources of confusion in estate planning. Many people are relieved to learn that creating a living trust does **not** trigger new taxes, deductions, or exemptions during your lifetime. You remain responsible for reporting and paying taxes on any income the trust's assets generate. Because you retain full control over those assets, the IRS continues to treat the trust as part of your personal tax situation.

For example, imagine a homeowner who transfers their house into a living trust. This change has no effect on how property taxes are assessed or paid. If you currently claim a mortgage interest deduction, you'll continue to do so exactly as before. As trustee (often yourself), you can sell, refinance, or even remove the property from the trust at any time. All income—interest, dividends, rent, or capital gains—is still reported on your regular tax return. During your lifetime, the trust doesn't file its own return because the assets "flow through" to your personal 1040, just as they did before the trust was created.

Looking at other assets, such as investment accounts or bank deposits, the story remains simple. Earnings or gains that these assets produce go straight onto your individual income tax return, using your Social Security number for identification. If your trust investments grow, or if you sell stocks or bonds at a profit inside the trust, that activity is taxed to you, not to a separate trust, as long as your trust is revocable. For most people, the transition is seamless: income, deductions, and tax rates are exactly as they were before the trust.

This brings up a common question: Does putting assets into a revocable living trust lead to lower taxes? The answer is straightforward—no. The trust functions as an extension of you for tax purposes. Its main advantage is helping your loved ones avoid probate court and manage your property if you become incapacitated.

Federal Estate Tax: Do You Need to Worry?

Beyond everyday income tax, many people worry about estate taxes. The federal government collects estate tax only on estates above a certain threshold, and this figure changes occasionally. In 2023, the individual exemption stands at $12.92 million. For a married couple, this doubles to nearly $26 million, as each spouse gets a separate exemption.

Let's look at two families:

- The Sullivans own a home, retirement accounts, and some investments, totaling $500,000. Their estate falls well below the exemption and will not owe federal estate tax.
- The Andersons have $15 million in real estate, investments, and business interests. After the first $12.92 million, their estate could face taxes on the remaining value.

Most Americans—including retirees, parents, single homeowners, and families with blended households—do not reach these exemption limits. Still, a few states collect their inheritance or estate taxes on estates below the federal limit. Some states start taxing as low as $1 million. If you live in one of these states, your estate planner or lawyer can see if those rules apply. These state taxes use different thresholds, rates, and exemptions, so specifics depend on where you live and own property.

Myths About Trusts and Taxes

Myths persist about living trusts and tax obligations. Many believe that forming a trust means your assets "disappear" for tax purposes or that you no longer have to pay estate or income taxes. In reality, a revocable living trust cannot hide or shield you from taxes. You are still the owner, and you must disclose income, pay taxes on profits, and follow all relevant state and federal rules.

Q: Does putting my house in a trust reduce my taxes?

A: No. Mortgage deductions and property taxes are unchanged. You continue reporting and paying as before.

Q: Will a living trust shelter my investments from taxes?

A: No. Dividends, interest, and gains go right onto your personal return. The IRS treats the trust as your alter ego until your death.

Q: Can a living trust help me avoid estate taxes?

A: Not for most people. Unless your estate is above current thresholds, federal estate tax does not apply. The trust avoids probate but not tax.

Building the right legal structure for your assets sets the foundation for efficient tax management. While the revocable living trust itself does not cut your tax bill, strategic planning with trusts and other tools can reduce taxes for your heirs in the future. There are practical trust management options for minimizing tax consequences. These fall into a different category and deserve close attention in the next part of your estate planning journey.

Strategies for Minimizing or Avoiding Taxes Using Your Trust

Understanding when taxes come into play starts with knowing how living trusts are treated. A living trust by itself will not erase all tax bills, but with careful planning, it can help cut down or even avoid certain taxes. Taxes most likely to affect families during life and after death include federal estate taxes, state inheritance taxes, gift taxes, capital gains tax, and tax on any income the trust assets make. Each of these has its own rules and thresholds.

A revocable living trust keeps you in charge of your assets while you're alive. Since you're still in control, the assets stay part of your taxable estate, so there's no reduction in federal estate tax just by making the trust revocable. The real benefit comes with an irrevocable trust. When assets move into an irrevocable trust, you give up control for good. This can remove those assets from your taxable estate, which is a powerful way to lower future estate taxes.

For families worried about federal estate tax, a trust allows you to use what's often called a "bypass" or credit shelter trust. Here's how it works: a married couple can set up a trust so that, when the first spouse dies, a chunk of assets up to a set limit goes into a special trust for the surviving spouse. This amount does not get taxed when the first spouse dies, and when the second spouse passes away, what's left can go tax-free to the kids, up to that same exemption. With federal estate tax exemptions quite high, only those with large estates run into these taxes, but state thresholds can be much lower.

Gift tax comes into focus when transferring wealth to others, such as children or grandkids. With a living trust, you can give away assets without bumping into gift tax, as long as you stay within what's called the annual gift exclusion. For this, you can give up to a set limit each year to as many people as you want without any tax. By placing gifts to different family members inside a living trust, you can spread out the gifts over several years and use up your exclusions while avoiding one-time large gifts that trigger IRS attention.

Many pay attention to capital gains tax when selling property or investments. A big benefit with trusts is the "step-up in basis." When someone passes and the trust distributes the inherited property, the value for tax purposes gets reset to the day-of-death value. This often wipes out unrealized capital gains, so the new heirs can sell the home or other assets and face less tax. It's most useful for family homes, vacation places, and stocks that have gone up in value over time. If a home worth $120,000 in 1990 is worth $500,000 when you pass, your heirs inherit at the $500,000 value, and if they sell soon after, there may be little or no tax.

For those who want to do more than just avoid estate taxes, certain trusts bring extra savings. A charitable remainder trust lets someone leave property to a favored charity while saving on income and capital gains taxes. The way it works: you move appreciated assets, like stocks or property, into the trust. The trust pays an income to you or your loved ones for a certain number of years, and what's left goes to charity. You get a tax deduction up front, income every year, and any capital gains the assets have earned may get shielded from immediate tax.

Generation-skipping trusts shape how and to whom assets pass, skipping over a generation to land with grandchildren. This can dodge large tax bills that would hit if the same assets moved from parent to child, then from child to grandchild, all in two steps. Spreading out wealth this way means more stays in the family.

Trusts with clear "bypass" or "spousal" provisions work well for blended families and second marriages. For example, a parent with children from a first marriage can set up a trust to provide for the new spouse during their lifetime, with the remainder passing to the children from the first marriage later on. This preserves wealth for all intended heirs while controlling both taxes and asset protection.

Pairing a trust with smart use of the annual gift exclusion, life insurance policies, and retirement accounts multiplies savings. For instance, a living trust can hold life insurance or be the beneficiary of an IRA, with careful wording to avoid hitting rough tax territory. Updating trust documents to match tax law changes is always wise to keep the plan on track.

With a well-built trust, families keep things simple, sidestep tax traps, and keep more for the next generation. Choosing the right structure and keeping documents up to date cuts down both taxes and legal costs, freeing up more for loved ones and causes you care about. Families who handle these details carefully see real savings in taxes and time while keeping control over how their legacy is passed on.

Smart Planning to Avoid Costly Legal and Court Fees

Families who plan ahead with living trusts often spare their loved ones more than heartache. They keep them out of the courthouse, away from slow legal processes, and save thousands of dollars in fees. Many people think of trusts only as tax tools, but a living trust's real power lies in how it moves assets without court. Probate court often charges a percentage of estate value for settling someone's affairs, sometimes running from 3% to 8%, not counting extra attorney bills. A home worth $350,000 could mean $10,000–$28,000 in probate costs alone, not even including delays and emotional stress. By moving real estate, bank accounts, and other assets into a living trust, families often keep every dollar for future generations instead of paperwork and commissions.

The key to these savings is aligning legal steps with smart organization. Many people create a trust but do not finish "funding" it. To really skip probate and all related costs, every asset must be retitled. For a home, this means recording a new deed with the county, putting ownership in the trust's name. Bank and investment accounts must officially list the trust as owner. Life insurance and retirement plans need precise, up-to-date beneficiary designations that work together with the trust (or bypass probate themselves). Vehicles, stocks, and personal valuables can also fall under trust control, though local laws matter for certain registration changes.

Setting up this web of instructions avoids court as each institution has everything it needs for simple transfers. Even small errors like a forgotten checking account or car can drag families back into probate for that single asset, causing new attorney visits and paperwork charges. To avoid this, most people use an asset list, updated yearly, as a core trust document. A detailed inventory gives the trustee a map and minimizes court questions later. Here's a checklist to steer clear of missed assets and headaches:

- Place all deeds, car titles, and financial records together
- Review ALL accounts and properties; if in doubt, list it
- Update the trust with any new assets after big life changes (moving, inheritance, sales, etc.)
- Check beneficiary forms yearly, especially after marriages or deaths

A living trust runs smoothly only when loved ones can find everything they need. Many families create careful plans but neglect to say where their documents are. Heirs may spend days (and money) hunting for a will in boxes, or arguing over which binder is up to date. The trust package should always sit in an obvious spot, a labelled folder in a safe, fireproof place, or with a trusted advisor. Sharing access and instructions with successor trustees or a backup family member keeps things easy when the time comes.

Naming a clear successor trustee matters as much as asset lists. Pick someone comfortable with paperwork, who knows family needs, and can communicate well. An alternate or backup is protection against accidents, illness, or family strife. Without named backups, courts may appoint someone and charge extra for the task, adding unnecessary fees. Along with this, give your successor clear directions: a contact sheet, trusted attorneys or financial advisors to call, and a single folder with every important password. This advice turns what can be weeks of legal back-and-forth into a process that takes only days or hours.

Mistakes that trigger extra costs often follow common patterns. People set up a trust but never record a new home deed. Accounts stay in individual names or are partly updated. The trustee may not know they need to inform each bank, insurance company, or title office. Some families miss out on "pour-over" wills that catch leftover assets and funnel them back into the trust. Without these steps, the very court drama people want to avoid comes back, and so do legal and executor bills.

Routine reviews take care of almost every risk. Mark the calendar to refresh asset lists, beneficiaries, and trustee instructions every year or after any life event, a sale, marriage, birth, or death. With a check-in plan, families keep their paperwork tight, minimize surprises, and stick to their goal of avoiding court. For more peace of mind, use easily found guides or checklists from consumer sites, local libraries, or trusted legal document services. Some offer fill-in-the-blank templates for asset lists and funding records that anyone can use.

With these steps, families give themselves more than savings but also speed, privacy, and peace for everyone involved. Careful trust planning means more time spent together and less wasted on legal fights, letting assets move smoothly, just as intended.

Final Thoughts

Now that we understand how living trusts affect taxes and legal costs, we can take confident steps to protect our assets and ease the burden on our families. By carefully organizing and funding a trust, keeping beneficiary designations current, and naming capable successor trustees, you set the stage for smooth transfers without costly probate or surprises. While a revocable living trust won't lower your taxes during your lifetime, smart planning with trusts and related strategies can help minimize tax impacts for your heirs and preserve more of your estate's value. Staying proactive with regular reviews and clear instructions ensures your wishes are honored, your loved ones avoid unnecessary expenses, and your legacy passes on as smoothly and efficiently as possible.

CHAPTER 8

UPDATING AND MAINTAINING YOUR TRUST OVER TIME

When was the last time you reviewed your trust? Do you know if it still reflects your current wishes and family situation? What happens if a major event like marriage, divorce, or a new grandchild occurs and your trust isn't updated to match? Many people create a trust once and then set it aside, unaware that changes in life can make important documents outdated or unclear. How can you be sure your trust will protect your assets and guide your loved ones as you intend? These questions matter because keeping your trust current is an ongoing responsibility, not a one-time task. This chapter will guide you through understanding when and how to update your trust, making sure every change is legally sound, and organizing your documents so they are easy to find and use when needed.

Recognizing When to Update Your Trust and How Often to Review It

A living trust is a living document. Lives shift, families change, and priorities sometimes move in new directions, so the trust that once matched your needs might not fit forever. When a trust becomes out of date, it leaves space for confusion, mistaken directions, family tension, or even the risk that hard-earned assets won't go to the people or causes you care about most. Regularly reviewing and updating your trust helps keep it as reliable and useful as the day it was created.

Major life events call for a close look at your trust. For example, imagine you get married or remarry. It's common to want your new spouse to become a beneficiary, share in certain assets, or even serve in a role such as trustee. Without a revision, a new family member may be left out or roles can be unclear. On the other hand, divorce or the death of a spouse means you may want to remove a former partner from the trust entirely, divide their share among children, or assign new people as successor trustees. This creates clarity and avoids possible disputes.

Adding children or grandchildren is another moment when a trust deserves attention. With the birth or adoption of a child, you likely want to name this new family member as a beneficiary. The trust can also add special conditions for minors, like naming guardians or setting up inheritance terms until kids reach adulthood. Skipping this update may mean new loved ones miss out on protections you intended for them.

If a beneficiary passes away, it becomes necessary to distribute their share in a fair and planned way. For example, maybe a sibling listed in your trust dies before you do. You would then decide how to allocate their share, like giving it to their children or dividing it among living beneficiaries. Careful updates keep your instructions current and lessen the risk of conflict or confusion for others.

Wealth and property also change over the years. Buying or selling real estate, starting a business, or coming into valuable property should lead to a trust review. For instance, buying a second home or a unique piece of art is usually a proud accomplishment, but it can fall outside the trust if not officially included. On the flip side, selling a property or business may mean a trust still lists something you no longer own. This puts your heirs or trustees in a difficult position. Making sure everything you want to pass on is listed, and everything sold or given away is removed, keeps your plan strong and realistic.

Shifts in relationships and intentions often call for updates. Sometimes people grow apart from a trustee or beneficiary, or a blended family forms after remarriage. You might want to support a new charity or modify your legacy to include community organizations that matter to you now. Any of these reasons are valid for making a change. With each update, you keep your intentions front and center and avoid unexpected surprises for loved ones or organizations you care about.

Staying on top of trust maintenance doesn't have to feel overwhelming. Creating a workable routine makes a huge difference. Setting a review schedule puts you in control. Mark your calendar—plan to check your trust every three to five years, and make sure to do it sooner whenever life changes in a major way. Events such as marriage, divorce, welcoming a new child, or buying a home are natural reminders that your trust may need attention.

Some people connect trust reviews with their annual financial check-ups, making it easier to keep everything updated together. Keeping a digital file with your trust and any property records helps you track what might need changing, while a checklist of life events or update prompts can keep you organized. When those changes do pop up, you'll have a clear guide for taking action quickly.

These reviews help prevent confusion and ease stress for your family. When your trust reflects your reality, you save loved ones from having to guess your wishes or sort out missing or outdated information. Regular attention keeps assets safe and ensures the people and organizations you care about are cared for the way you want.

Getting into the habit of proactive review means you are prepared to fix problems before they start. If life brings a change, the trust can keep up. Of course, knowing when to review or update your trust is one thing; knowing how to make your updates legal and clear is the next step. When change is needed, the most pressing question is how do you make sure your trust amendment is official, recognized, and ready to stand up for your wishes?

The Process of Amending Your Trust Document

Life events like marriage, divorce, or the birth of a grandchild make trust review necessary, but review alone is not enough. When a change is needed, amending the trust document makes your new wishes clear, protects your plan's validity, and prevents future confusion. Amending a trust is a formal process, not as simple as jotting a note or crossing off text. The law treats every word in your trust as important, so the path to making changes must stay precise and official.

A trust amendment is an official written document that changes part of your existing trust without replacing the whole thing. This approach works for clear, limited changes like adding a new beneficiary or swapping a trustee. If your changes are widespread, such as changing many beneficiaries, updating distributions, or rewriting the trust's core directions, it makes sense to consider a full restatement. A restatement completely rewrites your trust but keeps the original date and legal identity, making it simpler and reducing confusion for those carrying out your wishes later.

Steps to Amending a Trust

1. Identify the Change

   Think through exactly what you want to adjust. If you intend to add a grandchild as a beneficiary, state their full legal name and date of birth. For removing an ex-spouse, decide if you want to remove just one role (beneficiary, trustee, or both) and clarify this detail. When you want to switch your successor trustee from your brother to your daughter, be sure you choose someone ready for the responsibility.

2. Gather Documents and Information

Retrieve your original signed trust document. Gather any related existing amendments as well as the details for people involved in your changes, full names, relationships, and addresses if needed. If state law requires certain formatting, get a sample amendment form suitable for your state.

3. Draft the Amendment Document

The amendment should state that you are the trust's settlor, reference the original trust by its title and date, and clearly spell out which sections you want to change. Avoid ambiguous language. Write, "Article 4, Section B is amended to add: 'John Parker, born May 12, 2023, is a remainder beneficiary in equal shares with the other named grandchildren'" instead of vague language like "add my new grandchild." If you are removing someone as a trustee, specify the article being updated and name the replacement and their alternates.

4. Execution and Legal Formalities

Please print your amendment and sign it with the same level of formality as the original trust since many states require notarization, and some may request witnesses. If the original trust was signed in front of a notary, do the same for your amendment. Keep signatures clear and complete. Never staple or insert the changes into the original trust; instead, attach the amendment as a separate sheet at the end and label it as "First Amendment to the [Name of Trust]."

5. Organize and Attach Your Amendment

   Staple or clip the amendment to your original trust. Avoid keeping handwritten changes, as these are almost always invalid and create confusion. Only the formal, signed amendment is recognized by the law. Notify your successor trustees and key beneficiaries that you've made an amendment, and tell them where they can find the updated trust document.

Examples to Guide You

When adding a family member, your amendment might look like: "Section 3.04 is hereby amended to include as beneficiary Sarah Williams, born April 10, 2022." To remove an ex-spouse as successor trustee, you could write: "Section 5.02 is amended to remove Jamie Taylor as successor trustee and replace with Mark Taylor."

Key Mistakes to Avoid

- Never write in pen or pencil on your trust document, only signed, witnessed, or notarized amendments are valid.
- Do not forget to reference the specific trust section and use exact legal names.
- Attaching unsigned or incomplete draft amendments will not legally change your trust.
- Failing to notify the relevant parties can lead to disputes or confusion later.

State law determines if witnesses or a notary must be present. Some states allow self-amendment, while others require specific wording or more formal steps. Updates that change your intent for asset distribution or that involve large sums should be reviewed with a lawyer. If you are uncertain, ask an estate attorney to proofread your amendment for accuracy and compliance.

Keeping your amendments together with your original trust is a powerful way to guarantee everyone knows your wishes. As changes become part of your trust history, it becomes just as vital to consider secure storage and clear access for each document so no one is left searching when it matters most.

Keeping Your Trust Documents Accessible and Up-to-Date

Once you have amended your trust and made sure every detail is correct, the real work of protecting your plan begins. The way you store, organize, and periodically review these documents shapes how easily your wishes can be carried out, especially in times of stress or uncertainty. Only you can make sure no one is left searching, questioning, or second-guessing your intentions.

Keeping Your Documents Safe

Trust documents are only as useful as your ability to produce them when needed. The original signed copies carry the most legal weight, so keep these in a fireproof and waterproof safe at home or a bank's safe deposit box. Store backups separately from each other. If you keep the original at the bank, keep a paper or digital copy in another safe location such as your attorney's office or with a trusted relative.

For added protection, scan your documents and save them in a secure online location. Choose an encrypted cloud storage service with strong password requirements and multi-factor authentication. Services like online vaults can also notify you of attempted unauthorized access. Create strong passphrases and consider a reputable password manager to keep login details out of sight but not out of reach. For one family, this might mean original documents in a home safe, copies in a locked file at a sibling's house, and a digital backup accessible only by you and your attorney. If a disaster damages one location, at least one secure backup should remain.

Making the Right People Aware

Documents lose power if no one knows where to find them, or who is supposed to access them. Give clear, written instructions to your chosen trustee and any backup trustees, as well as to your executor. Share the storage location, entry instructions, and any passwords or safe codes they might need in an emergency. Handing over sealed envelopes with access instructions is an option if you want to protect privacy until the right moment.

Still, not everyone needs a full copy of your trust. Only the most trusted individuals such as your designated trustee or attorney should be handed or told about copies. Think of the process like a relay: you pass just enough information to the next person who will need to step in. For families, this prevents frantic calls and rushed searches for documents they never realized existed. If someone needs to act quickly due to illness or a crisis, paperwork is immediately accessible, not locked behind confusion.

Staying Current

A well-kept trust binder or digital file includes more than the trust itself. Life changes like new property, accounts, or family members —happen steadily. It's useful to keep a running asset inventory, updated contact lists for your beneficiaries, and current statements for your major accounts or policies alongside the trust. Create a simple checklist of what you keep and mark a yearly date on your calendar for a review.

When you update your trust, update every related document at the same time. If your trust now names a new beneficiary, your list should match. If you buy or sell property, update the deed references, insurance details, and valuations you store. File everything with the trust, not scattered in different rooms or devices. One effective approach is a binder divided into sections for each type of document, paired with a labeled digital folder with matching names and a backup on a second device.

Sample Annual Review Checklist

- Check original trust and amendments for accuracy
- Update asset list and attach supporting statements for each major asset
- Review and revise contact information for beneficiaries and advisors
- Double-check storage and access instructions for all parties
- Sync paper and digital copies to ensure all versions match

Organizing for Calm and Clarity

A straightforward filing system dissolves confusion. Divide your materials into these groups:

1. Original trust and amendments
2. Certificates of trust
3. Asset lists and inventories
4. Contact lists for trustees, beneficiaries, and advisors
5. Recent account statements or property valuations

Color-code folders or digital folder icons—one color per document group. Add simple, clear labels to each folder or subfolder, along with a brief table of contents or index at the front. Every page or digital file should show its section and date. Consistency lets someone else step in, find what they need, and act fast.

Organization is an ongoing act of care, not a single chore finished for good. Make it a routine, not a burden. Time you invest now means less chaos for those you love and a stronger safeguard for everything you have worked for. Every step you take to secure, share, update, and organize your trust brings peace of mind, not only to you but to everyone depending on a clear, effective plan.

Summary and Reflections

Now that you understand when and how to update your trust, the proper steps to make amendments, and effective ways to keep your documents organized and accessible, you are well-equipped to maintain a clear, reliable estate plan that reflects your current wishes. Regularly reviewing and formally updating your trust ensures your assets are protected and passed on according to your intentions, while careful organization and secure storage prevent confusion and delay for your loved ones. By adopting these practical strategies, you can confidently manage your trust over time, providing peace of mind today and a smoother future for those who depend on your thoughtful planning.

CHAPTER 9
TALKING TO YOUR FAMILY AND TRUSTEES

Have you ever thought about what really happens when a loved one passes and the family has to manage their affairs? How does the person entrusted with these responsibilities know exactly what to do, and how can misunderstandings be avoided before emotions run high? What if the very plan meant to protect your family's future becomes a source of confusion or conflict because no one talks about it openly? These questions highlight why clear communication about your trust is more than just a formality—it's essential for peace of mind and for helping those you care about navigate difficult times with confidence.

Communicating About Your Trust with Loved Ones and Trustees

A living trust is often the backbone of a family's long-term plan, but for many families, even hearing the word "trust" can bring a sense of mystery or worry. Breaking down the purpose and structure of a trust turns that anxiety into something more useful: a shared sense of direction and reassurance. Picture a parent sitting in a comfortable living room, explaining to their grown children, "This trust means that if something ever happens to me, you won't have to struggle with paperwork or wonder what comes next. Our house will stay in the family, and you'll know exactly how everything is meant to work." That kind of clarity grounds everyone. It creates trust in more ways than one.

Explaining these details in simple language helps loved ones understand the real value of a living trust. Instead of locking the legal documents away, open conversation can paint a picture of a future without surprises. The goal is to make sure family members are not blindsided by paperwork or confusion during difficult times. Reassurance might sound as simple as saying, "We created this trust so that the things we've built, like our home, my savings, and the family cabin, are protected. If I'm not here, you still know the plan, and that plan was made with you in mind."

Certain details should always be part of this discussion. Loved ones should know who is named as trustee, what their responsibilities are, when and how they'll need to step in, and which assets are included in the trust. Explain why each person was chosen for their role. For example, "Your Aunt Linda is the trustee because she's good with details and has helped us before with things like this." Connect each choice to familiar strengths instead of making decisions seem random. Talk through how assets will be divided, matching the legal language of the trust to real-life examples. "The savings account is meant for your college expenses, and the house goes to both you and your brother to keep or sell together."

Many families benefit from visual reminders. It helps to have a printed summary or even a hand-scribbled chart showing the main features: trustees, backup trustees, beneficiaries, and main assets. Laying this out together can lock in understanding that reading the document alone does not.

Trustees in particular must receive full and practical information about their role. Keeping a checklist handy makes this more concrete:

Core Information the Trustee Needs

- Location of the original trust and any amendments
- List of all assets included in the trust (such as the house, investments, accounts)
- Contact details for the family's lawyer, financial planner, and insurance agent
- Instructions for handling real estate (for example: maintenance, taxes, insurance)
- Passwords or digital instructions, if assets or accounts are managed online
- Backup trustee's name and contact information
- Calendar of key dates to review responsibilities or distributions
- Any letters of wishes or special instructions not spelled out in the trust
- Emergency contacts and preferences about health or property if incapacitated

Consider a scenario: A homeowner introduces their chosen trustee to the family lawyer during a relaxed lunch. "Let's all meet Attorney Ellis, so if you ever need help, you won't have to introduce yourself when things are stressful." This meeting, organized well before any crisis, removes hurdles. The trustee then knows exactly where to find deeds, titles, and even who to call for property taxes. The family also witnesses a united plan.

Timing matters. Bringing up the trust only during emergencies brings more confusion than comfort. Early and ongoing conversations allow the family to ask honest questions, express worries, and get answers before emotions run high. Start these talks as soon as the trust is finalized, updating everyone if anything changes—such as a new home added to the trust or a change in trustee.

Talking about these topics doesn't have to sound cold or like reading from a legal document. It helps to ground the conversation in care and openness. A parent might say, "I picked you as trustee because I know you're steady when things get busy. I'm sharing all the details not to burden you, but so you feel prepared." Invite questions, promise to revisit any unclear points, and let everyone know the purpose is peace, not pressure. Use clear, short sentences and avoid technical terms unless everyone understands them.

When families talk openly about these plans, they step into the process with less fear and more confidence. Sharing roles, reasoning, and instructions builds unity and prevents stress from boiling up later. What often disrupts trust administration isn't the plan itself—it's confusion, silence, or hidden expectations. The next step involves addressing how to clear up any grey areas or gaps, further cutting down the chance of misunderstanding or disputes.

Preventing Confusion and Legal Disputes Through Communication

Trust plans are designed to protect your wishes and prevent family disputes, but misunderstandings often start when information is vague, assumptions go unchallenged, or intentions are left unsaid. Sometimes all it takes for confusion to spiral is for one family member to learn about a trust for the first time during a stressful moment, or for a trustee to change a detail without explanation. People naturally worry when they're surprised or don't know the reasoning behind choices that affect them.

At the heart of many problems are surprises that catch loved ones off guard. An adult child opening a letter from a bank about their role as trustee, not knowing their parent ever set up a trust, can feel anxiety and resentment even before they read the details. Siblings may find out at a parent's passing that shares aren't what they expected or that a family property is to be managed differently. If we don't discuss these details first, such news frequently results in disputes, accusations, and long-lasting rifts.

Common Situations That Lead to Disputes

Tension often surfaces for several reasons:

- Unclear language in the trust leads each person to a different interpretation about their rights or entitlements.
- Vague explanations or silence leave loved ones guessing at motives and intentions.
- Changes to beneficiaries or distributions are made privately, then revealed later, causing shock or hurt feelings.
- Complex property, like businesses or vacation homes, brings unique questions and assumptions that go unaddressed.

Imagine two sisters who believe they will share their mother's home equally, only to find that one gets full responsibility and the other receives different assets. Without their mother's reasoning explained, suspicion builds. The sister with the house resents the upkeep; the other feels shortchanged. Suddenly, what started as an administrative task becomes a fight over fairness and memory.

In another household, a father talks openly with his children about his trust, explaining he wants each to receive support according to need: one has medical expenses, another is saving for school, and the third is established and receives less. By stating these reasons during his lifetime, answering questions, and writing notes to clarify his thinking, he diffuses resentment before it starts. The trust works as intended, and family bonds endure even after he's gone.

Clarifying Intentions to Lower Tension

Stating intentions openly changes the atmosphere. Rather than leaving beneficiaries and trustees in the dark, lay out your objectives and the reasoning behind key choices. Explain why some assets are distributed equally while others follow a different logic, like supporting a child with extra needs or honoring a family tradition with a certain property. These conversations, though sometimes uncomfortable, shift the tone from secrecy to understanding.

Organizing a family meeting can foster trust and facilitate communication. Use this time to:

1. Invite open questions, including tough or awkward ones.
2. Share the "why" behind decisions—such as the rules about distributing business income or restrictions you've set on selling the family home.
3. Write out the reasoning for decisions that may seem unusual, and keep these notes with your estate files.

For mixed families or complicated property, these steps are crucial. When a family business is part of the trust, explain succession, management rules, and what happens if someone wants to sell. If you've married again and have children from different relationships, consider discussing how you balanced the needs of both families. This prevents disappointment and legal wrangling later.

Supporting Trustees With Guidance and Documentation

For trustees, clear communication is a gift. Lay out responsibilities, timelines, and boundaries so they understand your vision. Make expectations concrete: require regular updates, give a timeline for major decisions, and define when beneficiaries can expect distributions. Written instructions eliminate guesswork and worry.

1. Provide plain-language checklists of trustee duties.
2. Specify how often reports or updates should be shared with beneficiaries.
3. Establish boundaries—such as not loaning trust assets or making side deals so no one feels pressured.

Direct answers to common questions also dispel confusion. Let everyone know who can access what and under which circumstances. If your trust allows for early payouts in emergencies, spell out what qualifies. If disputes arise, set out a process like naming a neutral third-party adviser so small issues don't turn into lawsuits.

Set up regular check-ins or updates, even informal ones, with both trustees and beneficiaries. A short phone call or letter reassures everyone and keeps rumors from spreading.

Lessons from Real Experiences

When clarity is missing, misunderstandings can escalate quickly. For instance, after a parent's death, one brother feels "left out" because the trust splits assets unequally, but the parent never explained why. Arguments follow, fueled by assumptions and old resentments. Legal fees build, communication breaks down, and relationships suffer.

Contrast this with a family in which the parent invites everyone together, explains each part of the plan, and then answers every question. She prepares a short letter outlining her wishes even for assets not detailed in the trust, helping her children understand and remember what matters most. When the time arrives, confusion is low, and the process feels fair.

Extra instructions, sometimes as simple as a letter stating personal wishes, guidance for particular items, or messages about values can go a long way to make sure direction is honored beyond the legal document. With this in mind, families find greater peace, and wishes are more likely to be followed as intended.

Using Letters of Intent or Guidance Documents for Clarity

Writing a trust involves legal rules, which makes the process clear on paper but sometimes confusing in daily life. Beneficiaries and trustees can still feel lost about what the trust creator truly hoped for.

Frustration or disappointment can happen if the legal words do not reflect the personal wishes behind them or leave questions unanswered, especially when it comes to sentimental items, pets, or special gifts. A letter of intent, sometimes called a guidance letter, serves as a plain-language bridge between the legal trust and the creator's intentions. Writing this letter gives you the chance to explain, in your words, the reasons for your decisions removing uncertainty, easing administration, and often preventing conflict.

A letter of intent is not a legal document and is not enforceable in court. Instead, it acts as a supplement to your trust. It puts instructions, explanations, and hopes in a format that trustees and family can understand without needing a lawyer to interpret. The trust lays out who gets what, when, and how. The letter of intent tells the story behind those gifts, clarifies gray areas, and provides guidance for decisions that may come up as the trustee does the actual work.

Core purposes of a letter of intent include helping the trustee settle disagreements or questions, offering reasons for dividing assets a certain way, and describing any special care for pets, dependents, or unique assets that deserve personal attention. The letter can also highlight your wishes for family values or charitable giving. Here are a few core uses:

- Giving practical guidance to the trustee when legal rules leave room for judgment
- Explaining the reasoning behind split or shared assets ("I left the piano for both of you because it belonged to your grandmother, and I hope you work out a way to share or rotate it.")
- Requesting that a family holiday home remain in the family, or that certain traditions continue
- Calling attention to heirlooms, photo albums, or keepsakes with notes about their history
- Asking that a cherished pet receives care from a certain person, with details about routines and needs

A common scenario involves a family recipe box, which has little market value but brings deep emotional memories. The trust may not mention it, so if it goes unspoken, feelings can be hurt. In a letter of intent, you spell out your wish: "I hope the recipe box stays in the family, maybe shared over holidays. I would love for each of my children to add new recipes." Or suppose there is a vacation cabin that has been with your family for years. The legal document might split the property in equal shares, but your letter can add, "I hope you agree to keep the cabin so you can build future memories together." These words do not change the legal force of the trust but give powerful context and guidance for sensitive decisions.

Common elements to include in a letter of intent:

- A list of items with sentimental value and your wishes for them
- Stories or reasons that explain the choices ("This necklace belonged to your mother, and giving it to you means...")
- Clear directions for the care of children, elderly parents, or pets if not set out in the trust
- Ideas for dividing shared property, such as rotating use or holding a drawing for objects not covered by the legal document
- Messages to reinforce family values, traditions, or charitable hopes ("I hope you still volunteer together at the shelter in my memory")
- Instructions about where to find the letter and how often you will update it

Plain language is vital. Write as if you are speaking to your trustee or children directly. Address them by name. Share the "why" behind decisions, especially if something could be misunderstood or cause surprise. Use kind, hopeful wording. Let your trustees and family know where the letter is kept, and remember to update it after major milestones like births, deaths, marriages, or large life changes. A judge cannot enforce the letter, but when trustees receive clear, heartfelt guidance, they often respect the wishes.

For those who want to avoid arguments and confusion, this simple tool makes a big difference. Taking the time to spell out the personal meaning behind gifts prevents second-guessing and reduces tension when your loved ones are already facing a challenging time. The trustee receives support when hard choices come up. Your relatives feel reassured, knowing that your intentions are clear, with your reasoning and stories captured for them to cherish long after paperwork is done.

Final Thoughts

Now that we understand how clear, open communication about your trust helps prevent confusion and conflict, you can move forward with confidence in sharing your plan. By explaining your intentions in plain language, involving loved ones early, and providing trustees with practical guidance, you create a foundation that supports everyone when it matters most. This thoughtful approach not only protects your assets but also strengthens family bonds and provides peace of mind for the future, ensuring your wishes are honored smoothly and respectfully.

CHAPTER 10

WRAPPING IT UP—YOUR LEGACY, SECURED

"Where did I put those papers again?" It's a question many people ask when trying to sort through a loved one's affairs after they are gone. Confusion over scattered documents can lead to delays, disagreements, and unnecessary stress during an already difficult time. Knowing where everything is, and having a clear plan in place, not only eases this burden but also protects what you have built over a lifetime.

Organizing your estate documents is more than an act of tidiness. It is a way to ensure your wishes are honored without confusion or delay. This chapter focuses on bringing order and security to your estate planning so your legacy remains protected, accessible only to those you trust, and ready for whatever the future may bring.

Assembling and Organizing Your Essential Estate Planning Documents

A trust binder, sometimes called an estate planning folder, brings together your most important legal documents in one organized place. Its main purpose is to make your wishes easy to follow, reduce confusion for your loved ones, and simplify the job of your chosen helpers, such as your trustee or executor. When the need arises, those managing your affairs won't waste time searching or risk missing critical paperwork. Everything needed is on hand, clear, and ready to put your plans into action.

Every strong trust binder starts with the signed original of your living trust and a few clear, readable copies. This legal document spells out what happens to your property and belongings. It appoints the person who will manage the trust, explains how debts get paid, and directs exactly who inherits what, and when. Having the original and a few copies ensures there's always a backup for court filings or when multiple people, like co-trustees and financial advisors, need access at once. For example, if you own a vacation house, your trust may say the house goes to your children, with clear terms for upkeep or sale. Without an organized trust and copies ready, delays and disputes can follow.

Next comes the pour-over will. While your trust covers the assets titled in its name, the pour-over will acts as a safety net. It scoops up any assets accidentally left out of the trust such as a forgotten bank account or car title, and directs them into the trust after your lifetime. For a property owner or small business owner, this is essential. If you buy a rental home but don't retitle it in the name of the trust, the pour-over will ensure that property goes into the trust, avoiding a drawn-out court process.

For control during life, two types of powers of attorney should always be included, each with originals and backup copies. The financial power of attorney covers everything from paying bills to handling investments. If you become ill or injured, your chosen financial agent can step in right away. This prevents court intervention and protects everything from your checking account to your rental property management. The medical or healthcare power of attorney lets a trusted person make medical decisions if you cannot speak for yourself. For families with aging parents or caregivers, having these powers organized and available means no one is left guessing during big life moments.

Add the advance healthcare directive or living will. This spells out your wishes for medical care if you're unable to communicate, such as end-of-life treatment or life support. For parents who want to spare their children from making tough medical decisions, this doc provides clarity and prevents family arguments. The medical team and your appointed agent get instant direction, avoiding unnecessary suffering or confusion.

A certification of trust, sometimes called a trust summary, belongs in the mix too. This brief document proves your trust exists and has authority, but it doesn't reveal your private wishes. Banks and real estate agents often want to see this before letting a trustee move money or sign papers for a property sale. Business owners or real estate investors use this summary to open new accounts or transfer property titles under the trust's name, all without exposing every detail.

Maintaining a current list of trust assets is vital. This inventory includes things like home and deed papers, car titles, bank and investment account statements, life insurance policies, and small business documents. Each entry should be backed up by copies of relevant paperwork. When the time comes to administer your trust, your trustee can act quickly rather than hunt for hidden accounts. For example, someone who owns a franchise can include licensing paperwork, making any future transfer smoother.

Beneficiary designations on retirement accounts or life insurance require their attention. The binder should have clear copies of completed forms and receipts or online confirmations. This guards against errors or missing funds, since financial companies will pay out based on these documents, not your trust or will. Suppose a parent intends that life insurance benefits go to a child's guardian; keeping the forms visible in the binder helps everyone stay aligned.

Strong organization keeps it all working. Use labeled tabs or dividers for each document type. Include a checklist summarizing what's inside and what's missing. Store a digital copy on a secure drive or in the cloud, using password protection. Back it up on a physical drive held in a fireproof safe. Regularly update both paper and digital copies whenever you change accounts, add property, or update wishes.

Round out the binder with contact lists for your attorney, CPA, financial planner, and insurance agent. Include copies of all current insurance policies. A list of digital assets—like online accounts, cloud backups, and social media profiles—and written login credentials with clear directions lets your helpers manage or shut down accounts as needed. For parents or caregivers with online photo libraries, password access lets memories stay in the family.

Storing everything together builds confidence and protects your legacy from legal confusion. This process also demands smart decisions about who can access your sensitive information and where everything is physically kept, setting up a smooth move into privacy and security planning.

Safeguarding Privacy and Peace of Mind in Estate Planning

With all your trust binder's pieces in place, privacy steps in as the partner to the organization. Careful recordkeeping turns into real protection only when sensitive details remain out of the wrong hands. Every person handling an estate leaves a trail of private data account numbers, social security numbers, passwords, insurance details, healthcare facts, and even physical property records. This information, if exposed, can invite everything from annoying spam to the nightmare of identity theft, drained bank accounts, or even scams targeting your heirs.

The kind of details that deserve extra attention include social security numbers, birth certificates, driver's licenses, bank account numbers, credit card details, property deeds, health insurance information, and logins for digital accounts. A shared computer, loose papers on a desk, or careless sharing can all lead to trouble. Identity theft remains one of the leading risks, often carried out when someone gathers enough information — an account number here, a digital password there — to impersonate a person, take out loans, or drain accounts. Addresses or phone numbers shared without protection frequently result in junk mail and unwanted calls.

A solid privacy plan starts with storage. Physical documents live best in locked, fireproof boxes at home. Safe deposit boxes in banks add another level for anything you rarely need but want to keep extra secure, such as original wills or property deeds. Make sure these are not left where visitors, cleaning staff, or anyone outside your trusted circle might glance at them. Share the location and access instructions with only a couple of people you trust absolutely, such as a spouse or legal representative. Over-sharing reduces security.

When it comes to digital files, create unique, hard-to-guess passwords for each folder or file containing personal details. Do not use predictable combinations - no birthdays, pet names, or repeated strings. Password managers can help generate and store complex passwords. Encrypt digital documents by using built-in file encryption tools or setting passwords for sensitive PDFs and word processor documents. If you choose cloud storage, pick a provider known for solid security, including two-factor authentication and strong privacy terms. Example: after writing your will, you scan and save a copy in an encrypted folder on Google Drive. Set a strong password, and only share it with your executor.

Access should always match your situation. If a divorce or new marriage changes your circle of trust, update who knows the combinations, passwords, or even the location of key files. Neglecting this step can leave former partners or even estranged relatives with too much power or trusted new people with none. Review your permissions every year or whenever relationships or responsibilities change.

Communicating safely matters as much as storage. Never send passwords, social security numbers, or bank details through plain email, texts, or social messaging. These can be intercepted or forwarded with a few careless clicks. When you need to transfer sensitive documents, consider these options:

- Secure online portals often used by attorneys and banks
- Physical hand-off—giving originals or copies to others in person
- Certified mail with delivery alerts for important paper documents
- Password-protected digital attachments, with passwords shared by phone rather than email
- Two-factor authentication for online platforms

Everyday habits also play a big role. Avoid using shared family computers to store or edit financial files. If you must, create a separate, password-protected profile and never save passwords or files to the desktop. Backups matter—if your laptop dies or your home experiences a break-in, you don't want to lose everything or find it's now in the wrong hands. But think hard about who gets the backup. Trusted adult children, legal counsel, or a second executor may be candidates. Avoid including unrelated friends or business partners in your backup plans to prevent confusion or disputes if something happens to you.

Examples cut through confusion. Imagine a woman who kept her trust binder on her bookshelf, visible to guests. When a neighbor's curious child opened it, a stray paper was lost and later mishandled, leading to calls from scammers weeks later. This could refer to a family that failed to update the ex-spouse's access to online banking, leading to the discovery that assets had quietly vanished following a sudden illness.

Privacy becomes even more effective when it's a family affair. Teaching your trusted representatives how and why files are protected lets them keep your wishes secure while responding confidently on your behalf. Walk them through the process of how to access files, who they can share with, and what never to communicate by regular email or social media. This reduces future mistakes and speeds up needed actions during emergencies.

Before your binder is declared done, take a moment. Review each method of storage, sharing, and updating to make sure your information remains safe. Keeping these steps in mind means your legacy stays protected from both accidental and purposeful threats, paving the way for the last checklist that brings every loose end together.

The Ultimate Living Trust Success Checklist

When every important document sits snugly in its folder, privacy turns from theory into real protection. Families who keep trust files organized and secure avoid chaos, lost files, and needless worry. Taking time now to double-check every step locks in peace of mind.

Step-by-Step Living Trust Finalization Checklist

- **Examine Each Page for Accuracy and Completeness**

    Compare all trust documents with the most recent information about your assets and wishes. Names, dates, and addresses must match exactly—spelling errors or outdated contact information can delay or stop your plans in court.

    Tip: Use a highlighter to mark spots you're unsure about and return to them with fresh eyes or with a helper.

    Even small omissions like a missing initial, unsigned page, or extra blank space can cause trouble for your family at the very time they need support the most.

- **Retitle Real Estate and Financial Assets to the Trust**

  Make sure each property has its deed clearly signed over to the trust.

  Example: For a family home, the county records must show the trust as the new owner of the property, not an individual's name.

  Do the same for bank accounts, investment funds, and business interests. Call the bank and ask for the trust transfer paperwork. Get all confirmation letters in writing.

  Common pitfall: Skipping this step leaves assets outside the trust's protection, often resulting in probate and argument among heirs.

- **Gather and Organize All Supporting Legal Documents**

  Place your will, powers of attorney, advance healthcare directive, property schedules, beneficiary lists, and any guardianship designations together in a single, clearly labeled binder or folder.

  Maintain both physical and digital copies whenever possible. Use password-protected files stored in secure cloud storage or on an encrypted external drive.

  Useful tool: Color-coded file dividers or folders make finding each document faster under stress.

- **Secure Storage and Reliable Access**

  Store original signed documents in a fireproof safe, bank safe deposit box, or locked file cabinet with restricted access.

  Choose two to three trusted people (successor trustees, agents, spouse, attorney) and ensure that they either know how to access these documents or hold a copy.

Do not rely on a single location, as disasters or technical failure can leave your family stranded.

• Keep Track of Digital Accounts and Access Information

List every online banking, retirement, investment, crypto, and document storage account attached to your estate. Write down account numbers and access instructions, and store these with your trust documents.

If passwords change, update the list immediately.

Provide clear written instructions on how to recover or access each account.

Tip: Use a secure password manager and include the master password on paper, sealed in the file for your successor trustee.

• Communicate Roles and Document Locations to Key People

Speak directly with your successor trustees, agents, and main beneficiaries. Show them where documents live and walk them through their responsibilities.

Give a printed "cheat sheet" with contact information, safe combinations, or access codes.

Avoid the problem of secrets—confusion and disputes can pop up fast when people don't know where to look or what you wanted.

• Set Up a System for Regular Reviews

Plan to revisit your documents every two or three years, and after major life events like births, deaths, marriages, divorces, new investments, or property sales.

Adjust property schedules and beneficiary lists as your circumstances shift. Use a calendar reminder or a checklist app to stay on track.

Tip: Keep a simple review log with the date, notes, and any changes made.

- **Document Every Action, Change, and Communication**

  Record when assets are retitled, passwords updated, people notified, or legal advice received. Write this in a bound notebook or a digital spreadsheet.

  This record will save time for successors who want to show that everything was handled according to your wishes.

- **Check for Complex or High-Value Asset Issues**

  Businesses, out-of-state property, intellectual property, or large investments might need a lawyer's eye. If anything feels confusing or high stakes, get a review from a qualified estate attorney. A small check now can prevent months of conflict later.

Sample Trust File Organization

- Living trust document (original, signed)
- Property deeds retitled to trust
- Financial account transfer letters
- Schedule of assets
- Will and powers of attorney
- Advance healthcare directive
- List of digital accounts and passwords (sealed)
- Communication cheat sheet for trustees
- Review and action log

Staying organized and proactive means heirs can skip headaches, speed through the legal process, and focus on honoring your wishes. Every item checked off secures your estate's future and protects your loved ones from confusion and disputes when it matters most.

Bringing It All Together

Now that you have a clear roadmap for assembling, organizing, and securing your estate planning documents, you can move forward with confidence that your legacy is protected. A well-prepared trust binder, combined with strong privacy measures and regular reviews, ensures your wishes are honored smoothly and without unnecessary delays or disputes. Taking these practical steps today means your loved ones will be spared confusion and stress tomorrow, allowing them to focus on what truly matters—preserving your family's future and peace of mind.

YOUR VOICE CAN SAFEGUARD SOMEONE'S FUTURE

Every step we take to plan ahead becomes a gift of peace of mind for those we leave behind.

Have you ever paused to think about what would happen to your family, home, and assets if something unexpected occurred?

Imagine a loved one suddenly facing complicated court proceedings, mounting legal costs, and unnecessary stress simply because no clear living trust was in place. Your reflections on this book and what you've learned about living trusts could inspire others to protect their families before it is too late.

If this book helped you understand how a living trust works, organize your estate with greater confidence, or feel more at ease about your family's future, I would be truly grateful if you shared a short, honest review. Your feedback supports my work and serves as a guiding light for someone who may be standing where you once stood—unsure, anxious, but ready to safeguard what matters most. Even a few sentences can ripple outward, helping others take charge of their legacy with clarity and peace of mind.

Thank you for reading, reflecting, and being part of this journey. Your words may carry more impact than you realize.

CONCLUSION

There's a quiet reassurance that comes when you know you've taken steps to protect what matters most. After reading this book, you're far better equipped than most people. You understand what a living trust is, how it can guard your wishes, and why it's one of the most powerful but straightforward tools for securing your family's future.

A lot of people worry about estate planning—some feel it's too complicated, others think they don't have enough assets to bother, or maybe they've heard horror stories about probate court dragging on for months or even years. If any of these concerns sound familiar, you're not alone. These fears are understandable, especially given the confusion that often surrounds estate planning and wealth transfer. But here's the truth: setting up a living trust isn't reserved for the ultra-wealthy or legal experts. It's an act of care, clarity, and foresight open to anyone who wants to offer their loved ones peace of mind and certainty.

The core benefit of having a living trust in place is simple: it gives you control. You choose how your assets are handled, who receives them, and under what conditions. Instead of leaving things to chance—or to unpredictable court processes—you create a clear path for your home, savings, and cherished belongings. For homeowners, this means your property can pass directly to your family or chosen heirs without being tied up in the probate system, which can be expensive, invasive, and time-consuming.

Middle-income families especially stand to gain. The costs of probate are often disproportionate to the value of the estate, eating into inheritances and delaying closure at a difficult time. With a living trust, those expenses can be avoided almost entirely. Your family won't have to deal with mountains of paperwork or pay out thousands in legal fees just to claim what you intended for them. They'll also avoid the public records process, maintaining privacy during a sensitive period.

For parents and grandparents, a living trust is a real gift to those you love. It's not just about money—it's about making transitions easier, keeping your intentions crystal clear, and even protecting young beneficiaries until they're ready to manage assets responsibly. If you've spent years working hard for your family, a trust ensures your efforts continue to support them, no matter what happens next.

If you're caring for aging parents, or guiding them through their own estate planning, the ideas in this book will help you ask the right questions and avoid common mistakes together. Acting now, before a crisis or illness, means sidestepping confusion and heartache later.

And if you're a young professional or small business owner just starting to accumulate assets: there's no downside to early planning. A living trust can be updated as life changes. Marriage, children, new properties, or a growing business—all can be addressed in the trust as your circumstances evolve. Starting now sets a stable foundation, giving you freedom to focus on the future.

Maybe your situation involves a blended family, stepchildren, or dependents with unique needs. Clarity is essential in these cases, where generic wills or intestacy laws (what happens if you don't have a plan) may not reflect your wishes at all. A living trust allows you to spell things out precisely, minimizing conflict and potential challenges after you're gone.

Throughout this book, we've broken down the steps to creating a living trust using simple, modern language—no legal jargon, no unnecessary technicalities. The process might seem daunting at first, but by approaching it in manageable pieces, you can steadily move forward. Remember: you don't have to do everything all at once. Even small actions taken today—making a list of your assets, thinking about your trusted decision-makers, talking with your spouse or children—can set the wheels in motion. Each step reduces the risk of confusion later and increases security for your family.

Many people put off estate planning, promising themselves they'll get to it someday. Yet the unexpected can happen at any time. By acting now, you're taking charge of your story while you still have every option available. You're protecting your legacy, your loved ones, and yourself from unnecessary stress.

Sometimes, the hardest part is just getting started. If you've read this far, you've already accomplished more than most. You've carved out time to educate yourself and demystify a subject that can feel intimidating or overwhelming. That's a victory worth celebrating. You've closed the knowledge gap, and now, you're poised to close the action gap as well.

You do not need to finish everything overnight. Set a realistic timeline; give yourself permission to go at your own pace. Perhaps you begin with a short meeting with your partner to discuss priorities. Or maybe you draft a simple outline of your wishes. Every effort counts. Over time, these small steps come together to form a robust plan—a safety net woven lovingly for your family.

If you prefer a hands-on approach and want to minimize attorney involvement, there are practical resources and guides available. This book's approach is designed for DIY-minded individuals, empowering you with checklists, sample documents, and explanations in plain English. You may find that, having learned the basics, you feel comfortable handling a great deal yourself and only need professional input for specific questions. That puts you fully in the driver's seat, saving both time and money.

If you do decide to consult an attorney, you'll be able to communicate clearly, ask informed questions, and insist on transparency throughout the process. That kind of confidence is invaluable, ensuring you receive the service and results you deserve.

Most importantly, with a living trust in place, you remove much of the uncertainty and anxiety that so often surrounds end-of-life matters. You give your family the enormous gift of clarity. No guessing games, no searching through boxes for forgotten documents, no family friction over ambiguous instructions. Instead, you leave behind a roadmap, tailored to your values and goals, that enables your loved ones to grieve, remember, and ultimately move forward with compassion and understanding.

As you close this book, take a moment to recognize your accomplishment. You've gained knowledge that will ripple outwards, benefitting everyone you care about. The peace of mind you create is not just for yourself, but a lasting legacy that will echo through generations.

Secure your future by putting your plan into action. Protect your home, your savings, your family, and your story—while you have the power and presence of mind to do so. Start today. Small steps lead to big rewards, for you and for everyone who depends on you. Peace of mind truly does start with a plan—and now, you have everything you need to make yours a reality.

www.ingramcontent.com/pod-product-compliance
Lightning Source LLC
LaVergne TN
LVHW020234210926
848481LV00016B/2208
9781970839098